More Like Christ

*A course of instruction for
teachers to use with young people
preparing for confirmation*

A. J. McCallen

COLLINS

Collins Liturgical Publications
187 Piccadilly, London WIV 9DA
© 1978 A.J. McCallen
First published 1978
Reprinted 1981
ISBN 00-599589-02

Quotations from Alan T. Dale, *New World* (1967) and *Winding Quest* (1972) are reprinted by permission of Oxford University Press.

English translation of the Roman Missal, Rite of Baptism for Children, Rite of Confirmation, © 1969, 1970, 1972, 1973, 1974, 1975 International Committee on English in the Liturgy Inc. All rights reserved.

Nihil obstat   R. J. Cuming DD *Censor*
Imprimatur   Ralph Brown VG
Westminster 12 October 1977

The Nihil obstat and Imprimatur are a declaration that a book or pamphlet is considered to be free from doctrinal or moral error. It is not implied that those who have granted the Nihil obstat and Imprimatur agree with the contents, opinions or statements expressed.

Made and printed in Great Britain by
Wm Collins Sons & Co Ltd.

More Like Christ

By the same author
LISTEN!
Themes from the Bible
retold for Children

PRAISE!
Songs and poems from the Bible
retold for Children

MY CONFIRMATION
A work book for use with
More Like Christ

CONTENTS

PREFACE

This book provides a course of instruction for young people preparing for their confirmation.

The material that follows is divided into two parts, an introduction for teachers in five short sections, followed by the actual material for the candidates in eight chapters.

The introduction for teachers provides a theological and historical framework within which the 'lessons' that follow can be fitted. This introductory material is not itself intended to be taught directly to the children. But experience suggests that confirmation and the work of the Holy Spirit are so inadequately understood that some kind of preliminary treatment of the background information to this sacrament is necessary.

The material for teaching concentrates on the following:
  a) on confirmation as the 'perfecting' of what was begun at baptism, with special reference to the need for each candidate for confirmation to re-affirm his baptismal promises –
    i) to turn away from evil and to follow Christ.
    ii) to live as a faithful member of the Church under the leadership of the bishop.
    iii) to grow spiritually in the love and service of the Father, Son and Holy Spirit.
  b) on the ceremony of confirmation itself, with special reference to
    i) the outpouring of the Holy Spirit at Pentecost which is made present sacramentally to each candidate in this sacrament.
    ii) the making of each candidate 'more like to Christ, the prophet, priest and king'.
    iii) the way in which this 'perfecting' of each candidate is expressed in various signs and symbols.

Throughout this course great importance is placed on the words and actions of the rite. There is also a strong emphasis on the need for each candidate to make an adequate response to the sacrament – in keeping with his age and experience. This is not to suggest that confirmation should be turned into a rite of maturity, as some people would have it.[1] It is merely to apply the general rule that every sacrament administered to a person over the 'age of reason' should be received generously and intelligently. Candidates for confirmation should therefore be expected to respond to this sacrament with a response in keeping with their age and experience.

Obviously this material will have to be adapted to suit the abilities of those under instruction. The early chapters (concerning belief in the Father, Son and Holy Spirit) are intended to provide revision material – although they have been carefully built round a series of texts specially chosen for their relevance to this sacrament, and it would be a pity to leave them out. However, generally speaking, the later chapters on the significance of confirmation and on the ceremony itself should be given priority over the earlier ones, especially where time is very limited. If sufficient time can be made available, it would be desirable to devote a whole term to the study of this material, during which the normal syllabus would be suspended.

Given this situation, preparation for confirmation could begin with a votive Mass of the Holy Spirit. The readings for this could be chosen from those to be studied in the early chapters of the course, especially the story of the first Pentecost. Then the whole course could end with a bible service immediately before the confirmation Mass itself: a suggested order of service for this is provided in Appendix IV. This emphasis on prayer at the beginning and end of the course has a very practical purpose, for it is based on the fact that the Holy Spirit is the one who first leads us to pray to God

[1] See the Introduction for Teachers, part 3 (pp. 15ff.) for a full discussion of the suitable age for the reception of this sacrament.

our Father, and there is no better way of teaching this to candidates than by giving them an experience of it in prayer itself.

Each pupil should have a confirmation work book, an exercise book or note book, which he can keep as his own property later on. In this he can write down the questionnaires which are given at various points in the text, and can put down all those items marked with a line in the margin (as is this paragraph), which provide a kind of summary of the material given in the lessons.

Sometimes a short introductory note is provided at the head of individual sections or sub-sections. These are offered solely for the convenience of the teachers themselves in order to make available background material relevant to that particular section.

Scriptural passages have been given according to the Jerusalem Bible or to *The Coming of the Kingdom* (R.S.V.), and occasionally to the Good News Bible. Reference has also been made to Alan Dale's *Winding Quest* and *New World*, and to my own *Listen!* The text of the rite itself is taken from the Latin typical edition of the revised Rite of Confirmation (August 1971) as translated by the International Committee on English in the Liturgy (copyright 1975) which incorporates the new English words of the sacramental form: 'N. be sealed with the Gift of the Holy Spirit'. It is from the Decree introducing this document that the following words are taken:

In the sacrament of confirmation the apostles and the bishops, who are their successors, have handed on to the baptised the special gift of the Holy Spirit, promised by Christ the Lord and poured out upon the apostles at Pentecost. With this, the initiation in the Christian life is completed, so that believers are strengthened by power from heaven, made true witnesses of Christ in word and deed, and bound more closely to the Church.

Hull,
November 1976.   A. J. MC CALLEN

Part One

Introduction for Teachers

I. THE HISTORY OF THE SACRAMENT OF CONFIRMATION[2]

The sacrament of confirmation has developed considerably over the centuries from being little more than a 'part' of baptism to a completely distinct rite in itself. The study of its development can therefore help to unravel what has been a somewhat complicated history, and so to describe the underlying purpose and value of this sacrament.

'IN THE BEGINNING'

Christ promised to send his followers the Holy Spirit, who would *help* them after his death and resurrection. At Pentecost these same disciples experienced an extraordinary out-pouring of the Holy Spirit, which made them 'go out to the whole world' full of a holy power and strength, ready to continue the work of Christ with complete dedication.

---

[2] There is a wealth of material available on this subject especially concerning the writings of the Fathers of the Church. This section does little more than draw out the main thread of development so as to explain the background to the new rite of confirmation as revised by Vatican II, see pages 8–11.

For a popular but much fuller treatment of the development of this sacrament see Austin P. Milner O.P., *The Theology of Confirmation*, Theology Today Series no. 26, Mercier Press, 1971.

See also especially Appendix I for the Decree, Apostolic Constitution and General Introduction to the Revised Rite. The Constitution, in particular, enlarges on the development of the sacrament in the Middle Ages which is treated very briefly in this section.

'EACH PERSON BECOMES A CHRISTIAN AT HIS BAPTISM'

However, in spite of this 'Pentecost experience', there is little evidence to suggest the regular use of a special sacrament of the Holy Spirit as distinct from baptism during the first centuries of the Church's history. Baptism itself was understood to be the sacrament by which a person was brought to the Father through the death and resurrection of Christ by the power of the Holy Spirit. Baptism was also the means by which a person became a Christian in all its fullness through faith and repentance. Baptism was the occasion when a person became 'more like to Christ, the prophet, priest and king'.

ANOINTINGS AND THE 'IMPOSITION OF HANDS'

People now point to the fact that the early baptismal ceremonies included an imposition of hands and/or a series of anointings performed by the local bishop, and see in this the foundation of the later practice of the Church. But these anointings (both before and after the pouring of water) and the imposition of hands do not appear to have been thought of as making up a distinct 'rite' separate from the baptism proper. The local bishop was present during the celebration of the baptismal rites as the leader of the local Church – as the one most suited to preside over the welcoming of the candidates into the local community. It was for this reason that he was the one who usually performed the second anointing of the newly baptised. It was not because his presence was thought to be required for the valid administration of a distinct sacrament. Later on in the ceremony it was for the same reason that the bishop also presided over the celebration of the eucharist at which they received their 'first communion'. Baptisms at that time were restricted to specified periods in the year, and especially to Easter time, except for those in danger of death. Dioceses, also, were smaller in size then. So it was not difficult for the local bishop to take a full part in the celebration of the sacraments of initiation in this way.

THE DEVELOPMENT OF THE SACRAMENT

It is not clear when the Church began to consider the second anointing and the imposition of hands as a separate rite and sacrament. The process of development in this matter was a slow one extending over several centuries. But the first stage in this can perhaps be recognized in the two incidents mentioned in the Acts of the Apostles (8: 14–17; 19: 1–6) where a distinct imposition of hands is performed at Ephesus and in Samaria upon people who have already been baptised—though a detailed study of these texts would suggest their relationship to confirmation as understood today is more apparent than real.

In the first of these texts Peter and John extend their hands over the people of Samaria after they have previously been baptised by Philip. This appears to have been a solemn ratification of what Philip had already done, and a sign of acceptance of the Samaritan Church by the apostolic Church in Jerusalem. Strictly speaking however this ceremony did not constitute their initiation into the Church, for this had already been accomplished by Philip.

In the second of these texts Paul extends his hands over the people of Ephesus after re-baptising them – they had already been baptised according to the pre-Christian baptism of John the Baptist. In this case the imposition of hands appears to have been performed in order to hand on to the Ephesians the gift of prophecy and the other special charismatic gifts, then a normal part of Church life and practice. Once again this was not specifically part of their initiation into the Church, but an additional rite of lesser importance.

Each of these accounts presents an exceptional procedure. Neither harmonizes easily with the practice of the early Church regarding the initiation of new members, as given elsewhere in the New Testament.

THE 'GIVING OF THE SPIRIT' TO HERETICS

More important in this context is the use of the imposition of hands to give the Holy Spirit to people baptised by heretics. It was commonly thought that such people did not receive the Holy Spirit at their baptism, and orthodox bishops frequently required them to receive the imposition of hands to give them a share in the life of the 'Spirit of Regeneration', when they became members of the 'catholic' Church. This practice was the cause of a great and lasting dispute throughout the Church, and in the end it was universally agreed that the Holy Spirit must be given to all people at their baptism irrespective of the state of the person baptising. But the habit of 'receiving' people into the Church with an imposition of hands for the giving of the Holy Spirit may well have made the use of a separate rite of the 'giving of the Holy Spirit' more acceptable.

A PRECISE ANALYSIS

It is not until the end of the fourth century that a precise analysis begins to appear of the purpose and value of the individual elements within the whole process of initiation. By the time of St Ambrose and of his pupil St Augustine, we find a clear distinction being made between *two stages* in the process of becoming a Christian. St Ambrose distinguishes between the 'regeneration' of a candidate and his 'perfecting'. The action of regeneration is performed at the actual baptism of a candidate 'by water and the Holy Spirit'. The action of perfecting a candidate is performed through the imposition of hands and a 'signing' on the forehead 'by which he receives a share in the gifts of the Holy Spirit'. Here at last there was a clear distinction between two individual rites, between baptism and what we now call confirmation. And if we add to this picture the fact that in Northern Africa, where Augustine was bishop, the imposition of hands was replaced by an anointing of the forehead with chrism, we have the basis of the sacrament of confirmation as we now know it.

Nevertheless the Church continued to follow her ancient practice of celebrating both actions within a single ceremony. And whether a candidate was an adult or a child, the pouring of the baptismal water was followed *immediately* with either an anointing with chrism or with an imposition of hands.

BISHOP OR PRIEST ?

As the Church expanded and baptisms became more numerous, certain practical problems arose. It became no longer possible for the local bishop to preside over the celebration of all the baptisms within his diocese. In the eastern half of the Church both the pouring of the water and the anointing with chrism (or the imposition of hands) was performed by the presbyter (or priest) whenever the bishop was not available. But in the western Church it became customary for the presbyter only to pour the water (and perhaps anoint the crown of the head of a candidate) when the bishop could not be present, leaving the full anointing with chrism to the bishop at a later date. It was this western practice of reserving the ceremony of anointing to the bishop alone, which led to the practical separation of the two rites into two distinct ceremonies performed at different times. And in this way baptism and confirmation, which naturally belonged with each other, began to take on a separate existence, and to develop in isolation.

'SOLDIERS OF CHRIST'

When the Roman Empire became 'Christian', the practice of adult baptism was increasingly replaced by that of infant baptism, as children were born into existing Christian families. In Italy, however, a close connection continued between baptism and confirmation in spite of the fact that they had become two distinct rites. Bishops were readily available in all the main towns and cities, and parents merely had to bring their children along to them for the customary imposition of hands or the anointing with chrism after their baptism. But elsewhere, for example in France, where there were few bishops and much larger dioceses, parents were unable to bring their children for confirmation soon after baptism. They either brought them to the bishop when they were much older or not at all. It was the problem caused by this kind of laxity that inspired a French monk and bishop called Faustus to compose a now famous sermon encouraging parents to stop being so careless.

Probably Faustus intended to do no more than this. Certainly he does not seem to have intended to break new ground in the theological understanding of this sacrament. But in his sermon he so distinctly connected the post-baptismal anointing with the idea of 'soldiering' that, whether he intended it or not, he laid the foundation for a reordering of the sacrament into a sacrament of spiritual adulthood – something it had not specifically been considered until then.

Faustus argued that baptism was a 'cleansing' of the candidate, which needed to be followed by a 'strengthening' through confirmation, which gave him an increase of grace and 'equipped him for battle'. In his sermon he made a comparison between the whole process of Christian initiation and the lengthy process of joining the army. 'Military service', he said, 'requires that a commander put his mark on each of his soldiers' – this could possibly refer to some kind of branding of soldiers. 'But it also requires that the commander equip each of his troops with arms suitable for fighting.' Faustus went on to argue that the 'marking'of the soldier was equivalent to the 'signing' of the candidate at baptism, while the 'equipping with arms suitable for battle' was equivalent to the sacrament of 'confirmation'.

This pre-occupation with the need for a sacrament of 'strengthening' some time *after* baptism also appears to spring from Faustus' concern over the weakness of many of those who had been baptised in infancy and had later given up their faith. In fact infant baptism has always created certain difficulties precisely because it is a sacrament of faith and conversion, both of which are lacking in infants. When babies who have not yet reached the level of conscious faith are baptised, they are baptised on the understanding that the faith of the Church supplies what is lacking, and in the assurance of a continuous growth towards faith from then on. Faustus and the people of his generation were among the first to come into contact with the problems that arise when infant baptism is administered in a widespread and haphazard fashion. It is understandable that he should have looked for something *after* infant baptism that would build up the strength of young Christians. But it is unfortunate that he should thereby have given the impression that confirmation as opposed to baptism was intended to be a sacrament of spiritual maturity. It was not so originally.

THE AGE OF CANDIDATES

In spite of all that Faustus said, most bishops preferred to keep the age for the reception of confirmation as early as possible. Even as late into the Middle Ages as the twelfth century there are records of an English synod ordering the confirming of infants within a year of their baptism. But the shortage of active bishops and the difficulties of communication across large dioceses made this ideal increasingly impractical. By the time of the Reformation it had become standard practice for children not to be confirmed until they were six or seven, and this practice was simply re-affirmed by the Council of Trent. It has in fact continued right up to our own century.[3]

THE ORDER IN WHICH THE SACRAMENTS OF INITIATION ARE RECEIVED

A further change in traditional practice should also be noted. Over the centuries the relationship between baptism and confirmation and the eucharist became steadily more ill-defined as a result of their development in isolation from each other. However, at least the traditional order of the three sacraments of initiation remained intact, i.e. baptism,

[3] Though not universally so – see Franzen in *Sacramentum Mundi* vol. 1 p. 408: 'In Spain, Portugal, and their former colonies confirmation was given shortly after baptism.' Recent practice, however, appears to have allowed these exceptions to disappear.

followed by confirmation, with first holy communion following both of these – a practice, incidentally, still retained in the standard discipline of the Church of England. Even as late as the end of the nineteenth century, Leo XIII had declared that the reversal of this order, and in particular the placing of confirmation after first holy communion, was 'not in harmony with the ancient and constant tradition of the Church or the good of the faithful'.

Nevertheless, there was hardly even a critical reaction when Pius X introduced an earlier age for the reception of first holy communion by children, doing precisely what his venerable predecessor had condemned. Strangely, no one seems to have suggested taking the logical step of reducing the age for confirmation at the same time to restore this ancient sequence. But as a result of this action, the constant and traditional order of these three sacraments was radically changed, and it is this reason which explains the puzzling order in which they are received today, when confirmation follows sometime after first holy communion, almost as an afterthought to be fitted in at the convenience of the local bishop.

VATICAN II

This was the situation inherited by the Fathers of the Second Vatican Council. The Council bishops shared a general concern about the celebration of all the sacraments. They were keenly aware that 'with the passage of time certain features had crept into the rites of the sacraments which had rendered their nature and purpose less clear to the people of today'. They also knew that 'the need had arisen to adjust certain aspects of these rites to the requirements of our own times' (see *The Decree on the Liturgy*, no. 62). And so they decreed that the rites of all the sacraments should be given careful scrutiny, and be revised wherever necessary. With regard to confirmation in particular, they drew attention to the need to revise the rite 'so that the intimate connection which this sacrament has with the whole of Christian initiation might be more lucidly set forth.' They also recommended that 'candidates should renew their baptismal promises just before they are confirmed'. Further they pointed out that it was fitting for confirmation to be given within Mass. The result of these recommendations was the revised *Rite of Confirmation* of 1971.

The new rite of confirmation emphasises the close connection between confirmation and the 'first stage of Christian initiation' (i.e. baptism) in two specific ways. First, as the Council itself recommended, the candidates renew their baptismal vows immediately before they are anointed with chrism. Second, it is suggested that they could very fittingly be sponsored by their baptismal godparents. Both of these gestures provide a reminder of the 'intimate connection' between these two sacraments of initiation.

The 'renewal' of the baptismal promises is something of a misnomer. Infants do not make any promises at their baptism, and strictly speaking their parents and godparents do not even make them for them, but make the baptismal promises as a sign of their own faith. Children who have not reached the use of reason are baptised 'in the faith of their parents', and it is the parents who show by their own profession of faith that they are ready and able to share that faith with their children. Nevertheless there should have been many occasions when each of the candidates will have had the opportunity to make these baptismal promises their own. And the rite of confirmation requires them to renew their 'baptismal faith' in a solemn and public manner.

The new rite also emphasizes the close connection between confirmation and the eucharist (the traditional 'third' stage in the order of Christian initiation). It recommends that confirmation should 'ordinarily' take place within Mass, and encourages candidates to go to communion at their confirmation Mass.

Finally, the new rite has revised the words of the sacramental form of confirmation. From the twelfth century onwards the Western Church has used the words: 'I sign you with the sign of the cross and I seal you with the chrism of salvation in the name of the Father and of the Son and of the Holy Spirit.' These words have now been replaced by words dating back to the fifth century to make the nature and purpose of the sacrament more evident. The new words are: 'Be sealed with the Gift of the Holy Spirit.' The Apostolic Constitution which introduces the new rite explains this as follows: 'As regards the words that are pronounced in confirmation, we have examined with due consideration the dignity of the venerable formula used in the Latin Church, but we judge preferable the very ancient formula belonging to the Byzantine Rite by which the Gift of the Holy Spirit himself is expressed and the outpouring of the Spirit which took place on the day of Pentecost is recalled.' In this way the revisers of the rite of confirmation make clear that they see this sacrament as a sacramental re-presentation of the Pentecost story.

A comparison between confirmation and the eucharist may make clear what this means. In the eucharist the words of Christ call to mind the events of the Last Supper, but they do more than this. Through the celebration of the Mass Chist himself becomes present to his followers under the form of bread and wine, and they are put in direct contact with the Last Supper. In a similar manner confirmation calls to mind the events of the first Christian Pentecost, and again it does more than this. Through the 'celebration' of this sacrament each candidate receives a share in the same Spirit of wind and fire that was poured out on the disciples at Pentecost.

By presenting the sacrament of confirmation in this way the revisers have carefully avoided falling into the trap of supporting several other popular interpretations of this sacrament:

– They avoid suggesting that baptism is a sacrament for babies and confirmation for those who have reached the age of reason, as some people imagine it to be. Though in practice baptism is often given to babies and confirmation to people who are at least a little older, baptism is far from being a sacrament designed for babies. In a similar manner confirmation is not specifically designed only for adults.

– They avoid suggesting that confirmation gives a spiritual maturity and missionary zeal *not given* at baptism, for this is equally incorrect. Baptism, not confirmation, is the sacrament by which a person begins the process of becoming like Christ the priest, prophet and king.

– In contrast, they make it clear that confirmation is the *continuation* of the process begun at baptism by which a person becomes like Christ and is filled with the life of the Holy Spirit. And they emphasise the fact that the specific form of the sacrament is that of a 'celebration' of the Pentecost event.

SOME CONCLUSIONS

Originally baptism and confirmation belonged together along with the eucharist in a single rite by which a person was initiated into full communion with the Church. In the beginning they were all 'received' within a single ceremony. Only later did practical considerations cause them to be separated one from the other.

As a separate and distinct sacrament, however, confirmation can be seen as the *perfecting* of the work begun in a Christian at baptism. It provides a powerful 'outpouring' of the Holy Spirit such as the disciples experienced at Pentecost, giving each of the followers of Christ an increase of strength and understanding to help them to follow in his footsteps and to continue his work as members of the community of the Church.

2. CONFIRMATION AND THE CHRISTIAN LIFE

The teaching material in this booklet provides a kind of 'theological' introduction to the sacrament of confirmation. But the importance of this theological preparation should not overshadow the equally important matter of the 'spiritual preparation' of those about to be confirmed. At whatever age confirmation is given, this sacrament marks a stage in the spiritual development of each Christian. It marks a growth in the spirit of prayer and dedication in each candidate – or should do.

Curiously enough this is often not the case in practice. Children who are only nominally Catholic are often confirmed automatically, simply because they are attending a Catholic school at the time of 'confirmations' and are of the requisite age. Some priests clearly feel that it is their duty to see that every baptised Catholic child is confirmed, whatever the circumstances. To them the delaying of the sacrament to a later date is tantamount to throwing a child out of the Church. In a peculiar way confirmation, the second stage of initiation *into* the Church, can thus become little more than the *last* sign of Christian life in a child before he 'leaves' the Church. It is true that the delaying of this sacrament for some children within a school situation can create problems with that small minority of parents who expect their children to be allowed to take part in 'everything that's going' even if they are non-practising. But this complication does not make the automatic reception of the sacrament any more desirable.

Some people still defend this practice on the grounds that each sacrament is a channel of grace, and the grace of this particular sacrament will not be 'wasted' on a candidate, even if it only has an obvious effect much later on. They say that the grace of confirmation may at least rekindle the last embers of the faith in a lapsed candidate. The theology of the sacraments would suggest, however, that Christ would not usually intend to use his sacraments so haphazardly. And significantly the people who argue along these lines would be much less happy encouraging the reception of the eucharist on these· terms! At a time when the Church is making greater demands on the parents of babies who are to be baptised, some kind of response from the candidates themselves at confirmation must surely be expected.

Certain minimum requirements need to be agreed upon – though they would have to be enforced with gentleness and understanding. It is a fact, for instance, that many young children in Catholic schools throughout this country do not attend Sunday Mass – largely, of course, because their families do not attend either. The older the child, the greater the proportion of non-attenders. Mass attendance might well be thought the most basic of all minimum requirements, but if this were so, then many children would cease immediately to be eligible for the reception of this sacrament. Moreover, the Christian life requires much more than this; daily prayer along with a reasonably unselfish life could be said to fall equally within the range of minimum requirements. Also, especially today, some measure of social awareness is highly desirable. If, for example, the Duke of Edinburgh Award can make quite demanding claims on an enormous number of young people each year, surely the candidate for confirmation could be expected to have shown at least a willingness to take part in some kind of charitable activity according to age and ability.

The young age of the candidates for confirmation has sometimes allowed people in the past to treat them as fairly passive elements in the whole affair. This is unlikely to remain possible for much longer, and with older children it already seems essential that they be given the individual option of deciding for themselves whether or not they wish to receive this sacrament. It would therefore be very suitable for the local priest or school chaplain to interview each candidate individually before confirmation to discover his own decision in this matter. With large numbers this interview might only be a brief affair, but at least it would provide some emphasis on the importance of the role played by the individual candidate himself.[4]

The Introduction to the Rite of Confirmation also draws attention to the importance of parents in the preparation of children for this sacrament. It says that the responsibility for initiating their children into the sacramental life is primarily theirs, and they are expected to play an active part in the celebration of the sacrament.[5] If the preparation for confirmation is done through the school, it is particularly important for the parents not to be left out. Too easily can the Catholic school 'take over' the religious education of children to the apparent exclusion of their parents. This is a danger that needs to be avoided. Parents can be involved in the preparation for the sacrament by means of a Parents' Meeting at the beginning of the course of instruction, or by more individual contact with their priests and the teachers, where this is practical. At least on the day of confirmation they should feel welcome at the ceremony and be encouraged to take part in it as fully as possible. Indeed, the Rite emphasises that the whole community needs to be drawn into the celebration of this sacrament, especially if this is to be done at parish level. Priests are therefore strongly encouraged to see that it is well publicised as an important parish event and not just a 'private' affair for the candidates themselves. Presumably fewer people will have to be confirmed at any one time in the future so that there will be the space in our churches for others to attend.[6]

---

[4] In parts of Northern Spain today a written declaration is required of each candidate stating that he wants to be confirmed and is choosing to receive this sacrament of his own free will.

[5] See section 3, pp. 15ff.

[6] For some suggestions about parish and parental involvement in the lead-up to the celebration of confirmation see Appendix V.

3. THE AGE FOR
CONFIRMATION TODAY

This is hardly the first time that people have asked what is the most suitable age for the reception of confirmation. It is one of the questions that people have been arguing about all through the course of the century. In spite of this, or perhaps because of it, the Rite of Confirmation (1971) is not decisive on the point.

'With regard to children, in the Latin Church the administration of confirmation is generally postponed until about the seventh year. For pastoral reasons, however, especially to strengthen the faithful in complete obedience to Christ the Lord and in loyal testimony to him, episcopal conferences may choose an age which seems more appropriate, so that the sacrament is given at a more mature age after appropriate formation' (Introduction, section 11).

Elsewhere in the same document, in the Decree introducing the Rite, attention is also drawn to the need to make more obvious the intimate connection between all three of the sacraments of initiation. This requires consideration to be paid to the original order of these sacraments which used to be that of baptism, '*perfected*' by confirmation, and '*completed*' by the eucharist.

Today confirmation generally *follows* first holy communion instead of preceding it. This anomaly only began at the beginning of this century when the age for the reception of first holy communion was lowered. In spite of all the obvious benefits which this change has brought about, it completely upturned the ancient order of the three sacraments of initiation, i.e. of baptism, followed by confirmation, and *then* followed by the eucharist. Even when confirmation was delayed to the age of seven or later in the Middle Ages, children still received the eucharist for the first time *after* confirmation, because they did not take their first holy communion until much later again. Many people are keen to restore this original order of events, but unfortunately each way of doing so presents its own difficulties.

Some people would be happy to see confirmation completely re-united with baptism, even if this can only be achieved in most cases by allowing priests to deputise for the bishop. This is not the impossible solution it might appear: some of the Uniate Churches have always followed the eastern tradition in allowing priests as a general rule to confirm babies immediately after baptism. Even in the Latin Church itself, general permission has now been given for all converts to be confirmed immediately after their baptism or reception into the Church, by the officiating priest.

Other people, however, consider that the radical upturning of the western tradition which reserves confirmation to the bishop is unlikely to be acceptable in the near future. They also regret the possible disappearance of one of the few regular occasions when the bishop is seen in the parishes of his diocese as the leader of the liturgical community. This is a fairly significant argument, for indeed only at confirmation is the bishop seen in one of his primary roles, as the one who welcomes his people into the Christian community, and is 'in himself' the centre of unity within the diocese. Possibly, however, smaller dioceses and the provision of Episcopal Vicars could help remedy this problem by making bishops present more often to their people, apart from the sacrament of confirmation.

Given the existing situation, it would be possible to place confirmation immediately *before* first holy communion, even within the same ceremony, at the age of 7–8. This would certainly restore the original order of the sacraments of initiation, but it would place an enormous demand across a diocese upon individual bishops. It would also add another burden on teachers, who already are fully occupied preparing young children for their first confession and communion. Under these circumstances confirmation would very likely come off a poor third best – as it often does even now, when it happens to follow immediately *after* first holy communion.

There is another important point to remember. If children receive this sacrament after the time when they have come to the 'age of reason', a new set of criteria come into play. Each sacrament requires a level of response appropriate to the age and ability of its recipient. Confirmation as a sacrament requires a response appropriate to *its* recipient. And if the recipients have already had the opportunity of living out their baptismal promises for several years, then they must be expected to give a suitable response of faith and of service. In fact confirmation becomes a natural occasion for people to express for themselves the faith which was professed on their behalf at baptism, and a willingness to *put into practice* those gifts of the Holy Spirit that are now 'perfected' in them. Indeed the rite of confirmation specifically requires this by demanding of each candidate a profession of faith and a renunciation of sin. Many people feel that even if children can make an adequate response to the person of Christ in holy communion at the age of 7–9, they are not so likely to be able to do the same in relation to the less personalized Holy Spirit at this age. Certainly the presence and the activity of the Holy Spirit is notoriously difficult to teach in the primary and junior school.

Bearing all this in mind, some dioceses in various parts of the world have chosen to delay confirmation until candidates are twelve or thirteen, or even older. Clearly this practice does not satisfy the original order of the sacraments of initiation, and this is a major draw-back. Secondly, it is open to the criticism that it appears to make the whole sacrament into the sacrament of physical maturity (on the eve of puberty) which has already been rejected above. But given the overall difficulties of discovering an obvious solution to the problem, this practice has at least the distinct advantage of providing young people with an opportunity of re-affirming their baptismal promises at an age when they are really beginning to be faced with the full challenge of personal responsibility, and before they meet the demands of courtship and marriage.

This solution also provides a healthy reminder that the process of Christian initiation begun at baptism is not something that is 'completed' in one quick action. The process of initiation is nothing less than the full incorporation of a person 'into Christ', something that extends over a whole lifetime, if not longer. The separation of confirmation from baptism can have at least one advantage in drawing attention to the need for each Christian to continue that process throughout his life, and to keep on reaffirming his baptismal promises until his dying day.

The age for confirmation therefore remains a disputed question, and likely to continue so. Those who place greatest importance on the existing tradition of the Church may well feel happy to leave things as they are, with confirmation shortly after first holy communion at the age of 8–9. Those who wish to restore the original order of the sacraments of initiation may well look forward to the day when it becomes practical for confirmation to be placed before first holy communion either as part of the baptism ceremony or as part of the first holy communion Mass. Those who prefer to emphasize the importance of the element of the 'response' to the sacrament will choose to delay its reception until candidates are into their early teens. None of these is ideal, each has its own merits. The notes which follow, however, have been prepared with the last of these options in mind, for use with children of 12–13. Obviously, therefore, they will need to be adapted and simplified, if they are to be used with younger children.

4. THE WORK OF THE HOLY SPIRIT

Some people have called the Holy Spirit the neglected member of the Blessed Trinity because so little is said about him in traditional Catholic theology. In some ways this may well be true – few people appear to concentrate their attention on the person and work of the Spirit. But in other ways, it is quite false – if we look at the scriptures, we find several ways of talking about the Holy Spirit, and together they give a very full picture of his work. Each of the New Testament evangelists and St Paul has a different way of describing the working of the Spirit. In addition, we can also distinguish an earlier theology of the Spirit in the writings of the Old Testament.

THE OLD TESTAMENT

In the beginning God breathed over the unformed world like the wind that blows over the sea. The word *ruah* which is used here became the common word for the Spirit, and not just in Hebrew, for the Greek *pneuma* and the Latin *spiritus* (and, of course, the English *spirit*) all mean breath, or wind, in the same fashion. This 'breath of God' is that which makes the chaos into something good and beautiful. It is the all-enveloping power of God in which we ourselves live and breathe and without which we die.

This same Spirit is also said to inspire people to take up a particular work in the course of God's plan for his holy people. The Spirit tends to come unexpectedly, and often descends upon the weak and the poor. Young David, for example, is only a child until he has been anointed with the Spirit of God, but then he becomes a great leader, able to take charge of God's people.

This Spirit also gives men the qualities of wisdom and understanding – qualities that are essential, of course, to kings and prophets, but also important to ordinary people, if they are to follow faithfully in God's way (see 'the Gifts of the Spirit' in Isaiah 11: 2).[7]

THE NEW TESTAMENT

St Matthew and St Mark almost seem to picture Jesus as following in the pattern of King David. They say that Jesus is 'inspired by the Spirit' and 'led on by the Spirit'. At his baptism Jesus is 'anointed' by the Spirit as a sign of his commissioning as the servant of God.

Jesus describes himself as being 'anointed by the Spirit', when he is preaching in the synagogue at Capernaum. As Matthew and Luke both point out, however, the difference between Jesus and David is that the Spirit was with Jesus from the time of his conception, and did not merely come to him, unexpectedly, as a youth.

During his life-time Jesus promised that he would send his followers a spirit of wisdom and strength to help them
   a) to understand what he had been teaching them during his time on earth,
   b) to grow in their faith and trust in him as their Lord and Saviour, so that they might follow in his footsteps.

These ideas come especially from the Gospel of St John. It is in this Gospel that we are told that the Spirit was poured out on mankind at the time of the death of Christ. Christ is said to 'breathe forth' the Spirit (see 19: 30) with his dying breath. And certainly from Easter Sunday onwards the disciples grew in faith and knowledge and strength (see chapter 20).

---

[7] It must be emphasised that these passages do not describe the 'Spirit' as a person distinct from the Father, and certainly not as an individual 'person' within the Trinity such as Christians would now consider the Holy Spirit to be. And yet these ambiguous descriptions of the work of the Spirit clearly provide a kind of foundation for the more developed awareness of the Spirit that we find in the New Testament and in later Christian writers.

At Pentecost, however, the promised Spirit was given to *all* the followers of Christ, and became readily available for all those who were ready to repent of their sins, to believe in Christ and to be baptised. The Spirit given at Pentecost was a spirit of mission and evangelization that drove people to the ends of the earth to teach others to follow their Lord and Saviour (see the Acts of the Apostles).

Finally we come to St Paul in his Epistles, where we are told that this same Spirit continues to help all God's People even now. The Holy Spirit helps us

a) to believe in Jesus, to pray to his Father, and to recognize his unselfish love for us
b) to share the love of Jesus with everyone else
c) to build up the Body of Christ, by helping all God's people to be united and dedicated in his service.

As this brief introduction to the work of the Holy Spirit may already have suggested, each of the scriptural writers tends to develop his own distinct 'theology' of the Holy Spirit. At times it is therefore not easy to harmonize the richness and diversity of their ideas. But however disconcerting this may be, it may be the only way in which we can express the incredibly diverse activities of the Spirit himself, who as we are told 'blows where ever he wills'.

5. THE BLESSED TRINITY

NOTE: The preceding section on the work of the Holy Spirit is quite adequate in itself without this further section. But systematic theologians have for so long emphasised the unity and equality of the Three Persons that they have for many people left the Holy Spirit in the shadows. A mere presentation of the work of the Holy Spirit as given above is insufficient to offset this long standing imbalance. However, if we turn to the scriptures, we find both the unity AND the distinctness of all three persons of the Trinity clearly emphasised. Scripture, in fact, almost suggests a kind of 'division of labour' between them! This short section merely presents this 'division of labour' in relation to all three persons so as to underline the distinct action of the Holy Spirit.

i) GOD THE FATHER

God the Father is the Father of Jesus and the author of the Holy Spirit. He is our Father and creator. We exist because he wants us to do so. He asks us to obey his commands and to live in peace and love in his presence. If we commit sin, we turn away from him; when we are sorry, he welcomes us back to him. All the work of the Church, especially in her prayer and in her sacraments, leads us closer to full union with him.

ii) JESUS CHRIST, THE SON

Jesus is the Son of God. He is the 'revelation' of the Father, and the 'giver' of the Holy Spirit. In a mysterious way God the Father created everything that exists *through* him (as if he were his 'agent' or 'servant'). But most important of all he was born in this world as a person like us, to be our teacher and our leader, leading sinful mankind back to God the Father, something he does especially through the sacraments. Jesus calls people to himself so that he can direct their attention to his Father. He reveals to us 'in himself' the God we cannot see.

iii) THE HOLY SPIRIT is the 'breath' of God the Father, blowing like an invisible wind throughout the world. Although this life-giving Spirit has been at work in the world from the beginning of creation, Jesus Christ gave a new 'outpouring' of the Spirit on all mankind through his death and resurrection and especially at the time of Pentecost. The Holy Spirit is the 'helper' of mankind, working unseen, but inspiring people to 'wake up' to the invitation of Christ, strengthening them in their determination to follow him and uniting them to live together in peace and harmony as God's people. This is why he is called 'the Sanctifier' and 'the bond of unity'. In so far as each of the sacraments offers us a share in the death and resurrection of Christ, they put us more closely in contact with the new outpouring of the Spirit which was achieved by Christ.

iv) Throughout our lives we experience the working of the Blessed Trinity. From the moment of our conception right through to the point of death we are called to share in the eternal life of the Father through Jesus Christ, his Son, in the fellowship of the Holy Spirit. The liturgy of the Church constantly focuses our attention on this in the Mass, in each of the seven sacraments, and in all her public prayer in which everything we do and say is directed to the Father through the Son in the unity of the Holy Spirit.

B

Part Two

Do You Believe?

CHAPTER I

'MY CONFIRMATION'

NOTE: The following questionnaire is intended to be written into the first page of the confirmation work book. Quite likely it will take some time in completion. Perhaps some of the details (e.g. re first confession), may not be known, but this need not cause undue concern. The date and place of baptism are, however, essential, and should be checked by a local priest or the school chaplain.

Regarding confirmation names. It is highly desirable for children to retain their baptismal names as confirmation names, if they are true 'Christian names'. But if a child wants to choose another name, teachers should make sure this is a *saint*'s name. It is also a good idea for children to find out something about their chosen saints so that they can make them their friend and patron as they are intended to be.

A SPECIAL NOTE ON SPONSORS

Many of the modern syllabuses place great importance on sponsors. They present them as exemplars, who will inspire the children to be confirmed to follow Christ better. They also strongly recommend that baptismal godparents act as the sponsor at confirmation, to draw attention to the relationship between baptism and confirmation. But this is not always practical and other suitable people, including the children's own parents, may present them for confirmation. The Rite of Confirmation (Introduction no. 6) requires that all sponsors be sufficiently mature for this responsibility, belong to the Catholic Church, and be themselves initiated into the three sacraments of baptism, confirmation and the eucharist.

Children should be strongly encouraged to find out who are to be their sponsors as soon as they can. Only one is needed, and though it is perhaps desirable for the sponsor to be of the same sex as the candidate, nowhere in the rite of confirmation is this demanded. Although the sponsors can act by proxy, it is much better for them to be present for the ceremony and to be with the candidate during the confirmation Mass.

(1) a) my name is . . . . .
    b) I was called after Saint . . . . .   [Christian name]
    c) I was born on . . . . .   [date]
    d) I was born at . . . . .   [place]

(2) a) I was baptised and became a member of God's family on . . . . .   [date]
    b)   at . . . . .   [place]
    c)   by . . . . .   [the person who baptised you]
    d) my godparents were . . . . .

(3) a) I first went to confession at . . . . .   [place]
    b) I first received our blessed Lord in holy communion at . . . . .   [place]
    c) on . . . . .   [date]

(4) a) I now live in the parish of . . . . .
    b) the priests who look after our parish are . . . . .

(5) a) I am going to be confirmed
       on . . . . .   [date]
    b)   at . . . . .   [place]
    c)   by . . . . .   [name of bishop]
    d) my sponsor will be . . . . .   [name]
    e) when I am confirmed, it will be . . . . . years since I first became a follower of Christ at baptism.
    f) my 'confirmation name' will be . . . . .

NOTE (1) SPONSORS

You need one sponsor to present you for confirmation. It would be a good idea if this person was the same as one of your godparents at baptism, but any other suitable person can take their place, including your own parents.

The sponsor must be a member of the Catholic Church. They must be baptised and confirmed and have made their first holy communion.

It is best if your sponsor can be present at your confirmation.

NOTE (2) 'CONFIRMATION NAMES'

It is not necessary to choose a special 'confirmation name' – the 'Christian name' you normally use can be used at confirmation so long as it is a saint's name. But if you do choose a special name for your confirmation, this must be a saint's name, and you should have a good reason for choosing it.

CHAPTER 2

GOD IS OUR FATHER

NOTE: In this and the following two chapters we consider each of the persons of the Blessed Trinity. A small selection of scriptural passages is given to illustrate the relevant topics. Each of these have been chosen because of their particular significance within the total study of the sacrament of confirmation. The various comments that introduce and follow these passages attempt to draw out their meaning.

Throughout these notes it is presumed that the vast majority of the candidates will have been baptised as babies. Clearly where a child or teenager has been baptised after reaching the 'use of reason' the renewal of the baptismal promises becomes much more a true 'renewal' and this would have to be taken into account. But for many children the so-called renewal may be the first time they have specifically heard of the baptismal promises. Hence the approach followed here.

At baptism the priest asks the parents of each child to renew the promises of their own baptism. This is the first of the questions he asks:

'Do you believe in God, the Father almighty, creator of heaven and earth?'

The parents answer: 'I DO'.

At confirmation the bishop asks the candidates to answer the same question for themselves, and they reply 'I DO' in the same way.

A. GOD IS OUR CREATOR

God our Father gives us a wonderful world full of beauty. As the following verses from the Book of Genesis (chapter 1) remind us, God makes the world 'a splendid place to live in':

27

Do You Believe?

Earth was a formless chaos
   lost in darkness
with stormy winds
   sweeping over the vast waters.
'Let there be light' said God
   and everywhere there was light
   splendid in his eyes.
     (from Alan Dale, *Winding Quest*)

The Hebrew people of long ago thought of this powerful gale blowing over the waters at creation as the very breath of God blowing life into everything. Christians nowadays would think of this 'breath' of God as the first sign of the Holy Spirit at work in the world making all things good and perfect.

The Book of Psalms picks up the same image and develops it in a vigorous and expressive poem, psalm 104. It seems to say that without the breath (or Spirit) of God we would have no life in us at all, and that it is fortunate for us that God does not take back his Spirit or we would simply die.

How many things you have made, O GOD,
   made in your wisdom,
   crowding the earth!
All of them look eagerly to you
   at their feeding times –
You give and they gather,
   you open your hand, they eat their fill.
You hide your face, they are frightened,
   you take their breath away, they gasp;
You breathe on them, they become themselves again,
   and you renew the whole earth.
     (from Psalm 104(103), Alan Dale, *Winding Quest*)

God the Father sent his Spirit into the world at the very beginning to make the world good and beautiful.

God the Father still sends the Holy Spirit into the world

even now to keep us alive and strong.

God *created* the world a long time ago.
God also *keeps the world going* now.

God is our Father because he makes us what we are.
This is why we call him our creator.

B. GOD IS THE FATHER OF HIS PEOPLE
God is called 'our Father', because he looks after his people
as a father looks after his children.

God the Father has a 'plan' for his people – he wants them
to *follow his 'way'* and to be a *sign for others* to lead them back
to serve God. In the Old Testament we are often shown how
much God cares for his people. He chose individual people
to be the leaders of his family, and to guide and care for his
People. Perhaps the most famous of these leaders was King
David. David was completely unimportant until God picked
him out from watching the sheep, and told Samuel to anoint
him. But when David, the shepherd-boy, was filled with the
Spirit of God, he became a great and powerful king.

The story is told in the First Book of Samuel, chapter 16:

One day God told Samuel to choose someone to be the
king. God said,
'I want you to find a new king for me.
I don't mind what he looks like!
He doesn't have to be tall and handsome!
Some people only think a man is good if he *looks* good,
but I can see how good a man really is.'
Samuel went to Bethlehem
to the house of a man called Jesse,
and he looked at the seven sons of Jesse one by one.
But he knew God did not want any of these!

So he said,
"Have you any more children?"

'Yes' said Jesse,
'You haven't seen my youngest boy yet,
but he's out, looking after the sheep.'
'Bring him here', said Samuel,
and Jesse brought in David.

David was a good looking boy
with red cheeks and bright eyes,
and Samuel knew at once he was the right person.

So he blessed David
and poured oil on his head
(to show that God was going to make him strong and good)
and from then on
God was always very close to the boy.

(from A. J. McCallen, *Listen!*)

In the story of David, Samuel 'anointed' the young boy with oil as a 'sign' that God chose David to serve him, and gave him the strength to do God's work.

In ancient times people often rubbed oil on their limbs to strengthen them before a race or some other athletic competition. In fact 'anointing' became a symbol or sign of *giving strength to do something.*

When we were baptised and again when we are confirmed, we also are 'anointed' with oil, and this too is a 'sign' that God has *chosen* us to serve him and given us the *strength* to do his work.

C. SUMMARY
1. Who is God the Father?
   God, the Father of our Lord Jesus Christ,
   has created us, and gives us life.
   He loves us all, and cares for us,
   for he is the Father of all his People.

2. What must I do to please God the Father?
   I must love God

with all my heart
with all my soul
with all my strength
and with all my mind
and I must love my neighbour
as much as myself.

3. If God our Father has created us and still takes care of us, then we, at least, should be ready to return the love he has shown to us. We can do this in our prayers to him, and in our acts of kindness to others.

CHAPTER 3

JESUS CHRIST

At baptism the priest asks the parents of each child to renew
the promises of their own baptism. This is the second of the
questions he asks:
    'Do you believe in Jesus Christ,
    his only Son, our Lord,
    who was born of the Virgin Mary,
    was crucified, died, and was buried,
    rose from the dead,
    and is now seated at the right hand of the Father?'

The parents answer: 'I DO'.

At confirmation the bishop asks the candidates to answer the
same question for themselves, and they reply 'I DO' in the
same way.

A. JESUS IS THE SON OF GOD

God is *our* Father, he is the Father of the whole of mankind.
But he did not simply *become* the Father of mankind many
thousand million years ago, when the world began. God was
always God the Father, because there never was a time when
God was not the father of the person we call Jesus. Jesus was
the son of God the Father, even before the world was formed.
In the Nicene Creed (the creed we use at Mass) we say that
Jesus, the Son, was not *made* like other people or like other
things; Jesus was *always* God's Son.

Because he is the eternal Son of God, Jesus is, of course,
very close to God the Father. He is perfectly united with him
in the Blessed Trinity. But he is also a *distinct* person of the
Trinity. The Nicene Creed employs a vivid way of describing

both the closeness and the distinctness of the Father and the Son by using the image of a light. God the Father is like a light that shines out in the dark (as an electric torch does, for example). Jesus, the Son, is like a light *from* the light (like a beam of light that shines from a torch onto the ceiling, making a distinct round shape of brightness, for example). The two 'lights' appear distinct, they *are* distinct, and yet they are also connected. You can see the 'light' of the electric bulb in the torch itself *and* its reflection on the ceiling: they both appear distinct. But if you look carefully, you can often see a 'beam' of light between the torch and the reflection on the ceiling, 'linking' the two together. Further, everyone knows that the torch 'makes' the light on the ceiling, it is the 'cause' of the light there. 'Flash' the torch around, and the light 'jumps around' as well.

This image is not perfect in every respect, of course, but it does give some kind of insight into the unity and the distinctness of God the Father, and his son, Jesus Christ.

Without the help of the gospels and St Paul we would not know about the 'pre-existence' of Jesus, the Christ, before his birth. Our knowledge of Jesus the human being begins with his conception in the womb of the Virgin Mary. We are told that the Holy Spirit 'overshadowed' Mary, and she conceived a child.

This 'overshadowing' of the young girl is the gospel writer's way of describing the unique conception of the baby she was to carry. The Holy Spirit prepared Mary for the tremendous role she was to play as the mother of Christ. The presence of the Holy Spirit was also a sign of the special intervention of God whose only Son was to be conceived within her. In some mysterious way this child was quite different from other babies. Every other baby that we know of starts his whole life at the moment of his conception in his mother. None of us, for instance, 'existed' before our conception – we began our life when we were conceived in our mother's womb. But with Jesus everything was different – he was certainly born, and born in the normal way like everyone else, but somehow the little baby that was born in Bethlehem was the same person as the eternal Son of God. As the Gospel of St John says, 'the Word was made flesh and lived among us'.

If possible, Luke 1: 26–35 should be read through at this point. The same passage will be found in *The Coming of the Kingdom*, no. 159.

B. JESUS IS THE LEADER OF GOD'S PEOPLE

For most of his life Jesus lived quietly at home with his mother, probably continuing the family trade of village carpenter after his foster-father died. Then suddenly, when he was about thirty, he began a new style of life as a 'teacher' and a 'leader', moving from place to place on foot, telling people to 'repent and to believe the good news' (Mark 1: 15). This 'public ministry' of Jesus began with his baptism in the Jordan.

On this occasion Jesus 'saw the Spirit, like a dove, descending on him. And a voice came from heaven, saying "You are my Son, the Beloved; my favour rests on you" ' (Mark 1: 10–11). Immediately after this the Spirit made him go out into the wilderness to pray.

Jesus later described this 'descent of the Holy Spirit' as a kind of anointing (see Luke 4: 18). And St Peter repeated the same idea in one of his sermons in the Acts of the Apostles. 'Jesus began in Galilee after the baptism preached by John. God had anointed him with the Holy Spirit and with power, and he went round doing good, and curing all who had fallen into the power of the Devil' (Acts 10: 38).

The New Testament story of the baptism (in Matthew, Mark or Luke) does not itself specifically use the word 'anoint'. But this 'descent of the Holy Spirit' was obviously understood as a kind of *spiritual* anointing even if there was no physical rubbing in of oil. It had a similar effect on Jesus as the anointing by Samuel on David long before. It *marked out* Jesus as the true leader of God's People. It showed that he was a kind of 'second David' and the 'King' of Israel.

The significance of the word 'anoint' used like this would

not have been wasted on the original readers of the gospels. In English the connection between the anointing of Jesus and the earlier anointing of David is not immediately obvious. But in Hebrew, the language of the Old Testament, it would have been clear straight away. In Hebrew the title of the King of Israel was 'Messiah', a word meaning 'the anointed one'; the King of Israel was not only given an anointing with oil (like David), he was even *called* 'the anointed one'. So the idea of 'being anointed' and of 'being a king' were very closely connected.

Incidentally the word 'Messiah' was translated into Greek, the language that the Gospels were written in, and became *christos*, a word which also means 'the anointed one'. It is from this Greek word, *christos*, that our own title for Jesus comes – Christ. When we call Jesus 'the Christ', we are therefore saying 'Jesus is the anointed King'.[8]

During his life-time Jesus was a great leader and teacher.

He gathered round him a small band called 'the twelve', who were his special disciples and friends. But he was also followed by an enormous crowd of other people, who flocked to hear him talk.

Today, long after his death and resurrection, we too can follow him

in the example of his life

---

[8] Later on reference will also be made to the anointing of prophets. Since this could cause confusion, it may be as well to comment on the fact here.

In some ways the idea of Kingship and of Prophecy in Israel are not as distinct as later thought would suggest. Some of the early prophets were political leaders in their own right; and both David and Solomon, the most famous of all the kings, fulfilled a kind of prophetic role at times.

It is probably helpful to distinguish the differences between the two especially for teaching purposes (see chapter 7(A) below). But since Christ joined both roles perfectly in himself, these distinctions are not always easy to maintain.

in his words and his teaching and
in the example of his death and resurrection.

We can follow the example of his life:
Jesus did not spend his life 'pleasing himself'. He had a
happy life in many ways, but he spent his time caring for
others rather than looking after himself.

We can follow his words and his teaching:
Jesus taught people how to live, how to be at peace with
God and with each other.

We can follow the example of his death and resurrection:
Jesus died because people turned against him. He died
because people were selfish and sinful.

But God was pleased with the love and dedication which
Jesus showed throughout his life, and he raised his Son to
life again, to show that sin cannot overpower the strength
of God. We can be sure that with this same strength
behind us we can 'rise up' above our own selfishness, and
live more like Christ himself.

If we follow the example and the teaching of Christ, we will
be able to take part in fulfilling God's plan for us and for our
world. We will be able to make the Kingdom of God grow
until it is perfect. Then we will help prepare for that time
when Christ will come again in glory, when everyone will be
able to see that he is indeed the King of the Universe.[9]

C. SUMMARY

1. Who is Jesus Christ our Lord?
   Jesus Christ is the Son of God,
   he always was the Father's Son,
   but he was born on earth and died for us
   so that we might be raised up from our sins
   and share his life with God for ever.

[9] This section does not set out to provide a complete analysis of the
work of Christ and is deliberately selective. Along with the other early
chapters in this book, it is intended only as revision.

2. Dying you destroyed our death,
   Rising you restored our life,
   Lord Jesus come in glory.
3. Day by Day,
   O dear Lord, three things I pray,
   to see thee more clearly,
   love thee more dearly,
   follow thee more nearly,
   day by day.
4. If Jesus has suffered and died for us,
   then we at least should be ready to get to know him better
   and to follow him.

CHAPTER 4

THE HOLY SPIRIT IS
OUR HELPER AND GUIDE

At baptism the priest asks the parents of each child to renew
the promises of their own baptism. This is the third of the
questions he asks:
  'Do you believe in the Holy Spirit?'
  The parents reply: 'I DO'.

At confirmation the bishop asks the candidates to answer the
same questions for themselves. Because confirmation is the
special 'sacrament of the Holy Spirit', he asks this question
in a slightly different way, as follows:

  'Do you believe in the Holy Spirit,
  the Lord, and giver of life,
  who came upon the apostles at Pentecost
  and today is given to you sacramentally in confirmation?'

  The candidates reply: 'I DO'.

A. THE PROMISE OF THE HOLY SPIRIT
Several examples of the work of the Holy Spirit have already
been given in the two previous chapters:
  The Holy Spirit at work in creation.
  The Holy Spirit at the anointing of the boy David.
  The Holy Spirit at the conception of Christ.
  The Holy Spirit at the baptism of Christ.
  These texts show some of the ways in which the Spirit
works. But there is one further important way in which the
Spirit is said to help people. In the Old Testament this Spirit
is 'given' in a special way to certain chosen people to help
them to *understand* the word of God, and to pass it on to

others. These people are the 'prophets' of the Old Testament. These prophets were said to be 'inspired', because the Holy Spirit made them 'sensitive' to whatever God wanted – though, in fact, they sometimes had great difficulty getting other people to follow God as faithfully as they did themselves.

The next passage comes from the Book of Isaiah chapter 61. Here the prophet has 'good news' for God's People. They have just been through great suffering and trouble, and God wants them to know that he has not forgotten them, and promises to take good care of them in future.

> The Spirit of the Lord has been given to me.
> The Lord has anointed me.
> He has sent me to bring good news to the poor,
> and to care for the broken-hearted;
> to proclaim liberty to captives,
> freedom to those in prison;
> to comfort those who are full of tears
> and bring them
> > happiness in place of sadness
> > joy in place of mourning,
> > and praise in place of despondency.
> > > (freely adapted from the Jerusalem Bible)

During his life-time, Jesus promised to send this same Spirit to his followers
> to strengthen them in their faith in him as their Lord,
> to guide them to understand and follow his teaching.

The story of this promise is given in the Gospel of John chapter 16:

One day Jesus said,
'The man who loves me will take what I say seriously.
Then my Father will love him, and we both will come to him,
and make our home in his heart.

The man who has no love for me doesn't bother about
anything I say.

I have talked to you like this, while I am still with you.
But later, the "Helper", the Spirit of God, whom the
Father will send in my name, he will explain everything to
you, and call back to your minds all that I have said to you,
but which you did not understand at the time.'

(adapted from Alan Dale, *New World*)

In this passage the Holy Spirit is called the 'Helper' which
is probably the simplest title to give him. In other translations
he is called 'the Paraclete' or 'the Advocate'. He is called by
these technical names because, like an advocate or barrister
at court, he defends the innocence of Christ. At his trial
Christ was found *guilty*, and sentenced to death. But the Holy
Spirit helped the disciples of Christ to regain their *faith* in
him, and to *recognize* that he was the innocent victim of other
people's greed and selfishness.

B. AFTER THE RESURRECTION

After the resurrection Christ gave his disciples the gift of the
Holy Spirit as he had promised them.

He came to them while they were still hiding in the Upper
Room on the first Easter Sunday. He came into the room and
said 'Peace be with you' and showed them his hands and his
side. Then he 'breathed' on them, and said 'Receive the Holy
Spirit'.[10]

This 'gift of the Holy Spirit' was made to the disciples to
help them in their work of bringing others back to God. The
early followers of Christ were like the prophets of old: they
were more sensitive to God's voice than other people, who
had become 'deaf' to God's voice because of their sinfulness.
The disciples had the task of bringing people back to God the
Father through the forgiveness of their sins. In this way Jesus

[10] Note the use of the word 'breath' in reference to the Holy Spirit who
is the 'breath of life'.

gave his followers a share in his work so that they could help sinful people to come back to God just as he had done. He 'commissioned' them to continue his work.

(See John 20: 19–23 for the story of this first appearance of Christ to his disciples. See also *The Coming of the Kingdom*, no. 285.)

C. PENTECOST

NOTE: The situation before and after Pentecost is sometimes presented in terms of a total transformation of the apostles from weak fearful people into leaders of enormous strength. This idea of a sudden change is attractive and memorable (especially for teaching purposes), but it is less than accurate.

It is not true that the disciples were *afraid* immediately before Pentecost. We are told that after the ascension they 'returned to Jerusalem with great joy, and were continually in the Temple, blessing God' (Luke 24: 52–3). It seems more likely they came together on the occasion of this Jewish feast to *pray* for the guidance and direction of God. In this situation they were *not afraid, but rather 'in waiting'*, praying trustfully for the certain guidance of God.

After the descent of the Holy Spirit there was undoubtedly a granting of extra-ordinary 'gifts' of the Spirit in a way that left a deep impression on the people who were gathered in Jerusalem. But the main significance of Pentecost was the generosity of the outpouring of the Spirit on so many people rather than the gifts themselves. Pentecost marked the beginning of the Church as a world-wide community.[11]

This way of looking at the Pentecost story can be particularly helpful during the instruction of candidates for confirmation. It provides a healthy emphasis on the need for *prayer* in preparation for the reception of this sacrament. The apostles prepared for their 'confirmation' by prayer, and the candidates, too, must pray for

[11] However the possibility of the giving of charismatic gifts on the occasion of confirmation cannot simply be excluded. Already the brief but remarkable history of the Catholic pentecostal movement suggests that it is not impossible for these special 'gifts of the Spirit' to be 'poured out' once more on occasions like this, given the right circumstances.

the guidance of the Spirit. Although confirmation is a sacrament, the effect of its grace can be severely restricted by the way people approach it.

This more scriptural interpretation can also help to take away the sense of unreality that sometimes accompanies this sacrament. Many candidates find it difficult to relate to the old idea of a sudden change in the disciples from weaklings into giants. Many of them would hardly think of themselves as 'fearful weaklings' previous to the reception of this sacrament, and no one could blame them for experiencing a sense of anti-climax afterwards if they were led to expect an immediate visible transformation in themselves and were disappointed.

What is more important is that they recognize Pentecost as the beginning of the Church as we know it. Then they should see more clearly that when they 're-live' the Pentecost story at confirmation, they receive an increase of strength to help them share in the life and mission of the Church community like the apostles. This 'strength' may not be given in a spectacular manner, but it is no less real for that.

The new words of the 'form' of this sacrament tie it ever more closely than before to the Pentecost story. It is therefore essential that each candidate knows this story with understanding.

When Christ returned to the disciples after the resurrection, he made it clear to them that they were to continue the work he had begun. Under his guidance they grew in understanding and confidence right up to the time when he ascended into heaven.

After the ascension the disciples stayed together in Jerusalem to prepare themselves for the task ahead by prayer, asking God to give them his continued help and guidance. Then at Pentecost, on this important Jewish feast, God answered their prayers, and 'poured out' on them the Holy Spirit of power – as Christ himself had promised them.

This 'outpouring of the Holy Spirit' had an astonishing effect, and the disciples were able to draw many people to Christ. Pentecost, indeed, was the formal beginning of the Church as we know it.

In the Upper Room on the day of the resurrection when Christ had first appeared to his disciples, he gave the Holy Spirit to a very small group of his closest friends when he 'breathed' on them. But at Pentecost this same Holy Spirit was given to a vast crowd of people. It was given to all those who were willing

to turn away from their sinfulness
to believe in Christ as their Lord and Saviour and
to be baptised.

Furthermore, all those who 'received the Spirit' were given a share in the work of Christ and his apostles. The Holy Spirit made them all 'more like to Christ' so that they could continue in his footsteps, and help other people to love and serve God the Father.

Before Pentecost: the disciples prayed to God the Father for help and guidance.

At Pentecost: God the Father 'poured out the gift of the Holy Spirit' on the disciples to give them the power and the strength that Jesus had promised them.

After Pentecost: The disciples began to do what Christ himself had done. They became 'more like Christ', ready and able to continue his work in the world as members of the community of the Church.

'It was now the time of the Feast of Pentecost, the Fiftieth day, when Jewish people remember how Moses gave them the Law of God on Mount Sinai.

The friends of Jesus were together in the house where they were staying. Then it happened! Suddenly, as if a storm of wind and fire burst upon them, they were all filled with the Spirit of God's power, and they began to speak in many strange ways. With the power of God behind them, they began to speak out boldly.

Jewish pilgrims from lands all over the world were staying in the city that day. They came from
Mesopotamia in the east,

from the shores of the Black Sea in the north,
from Egypt in the south
and even from Rome in the west.
A great crowd gathered, talking excitedly. They were
amazed, and didn't know what to think. Then Peter stood
up and began to speak.
"Do you remember these words from the Bible?
In the days that are to be
I will give my Spirit to everyone.
Your people shall understand me.
Your old men shall dream dreams,
your young men shall see visions.
Even to slaves
I will pour out my Spirit!" '

Acts chapter 2,
adapted from Alan Dale, *New World*

At Pentecost the Holy Spirit was experienced as a Spirit of
power and strength, driving people to the ends of the earth
to carry the message of the gospel. In the sacrament of
baptism and confirmation each candidate receives *a share* in
this 'power' of the Holy Spirit; each person is called to accept
his own vocation to take his part in the work of Christ.

D. THE SPIRIT OF WIND AND FIRE
NOTE: The Pentecost Spirit is described in terms of the images of
wind and of fire, two images which have often been used to
describe the power of the God of strength, who is so often 'unseen'
by human eyes. The following section is a continuation of the
previous one, and could easily be incorporated into it. It suggests
some of the ways in which these images can still effectively be
used in talking about the work of the Holy Spirit today.

Both wind and fire have often been used, especially in the
Old Testament, to describe the 'invisible' power of God.
There is a fairly obvious reason for this. Wind and fire are
both 'invisible' sources of power.

People who live in a more simple society than our own and who live 'face to face with the elements' are very conscious of the power of both wind and fire. They are aware that they meddle with them at their peril. They know that both can be put to good purpose, but they can both also be the cause of terrible damage.

Fire and wind have often been thought of as mysterious 'insubstantial' things. Fire burns with a flickering flame that is hard to follow. It 'leaps about' in the hearth with a life all of its own. Or again it can 'disappear' into the red embers of coal or wood, and seem to have 'died', only to spring to life again when more fuel is added. Wind is very similar. You can only see other things being blown by it, or feel its gusts rushing against your body on a blustery day. You cannot 'see' it directly, you can only see 'signs' of its power and its strength. Neither fire nor wind are 'solid' things. And yet they are just as 'real' as anything that is 'solid' – in some ways more so, as anyone knows who has been out at sea in a gale, or watched a large building on fire.

For reasons like this we find these images of wind and fire used frequently in the Old Testament to describe the invisible power of God.

We are told that Moses 'met' God in the form of a fierce, blazing fire, burning in a bush that was too hot to be approached closely (see Exodus chapter 3). Abraham 'met' God in the form of a blazing torch that came down from the sky, burning up his offerings (see Genesis chapter 15). Elijah 'heard' God in the form of a gentle whispering breeze up in the mountains (see Kings chapter 19). The psalms talk of God in terms of a roaring gale, sweeping through the world, often with devastating effect (see psalms 18: 10–15, 78: 26, 83: 13, 104: 3, etc.). The use of all these images reminds us of the powerful presence of the invisible God. He may appear 'insubstantial' to some people, but they are mistaken in thinking this. Both of these images also remind us that it is not necessary to be visible to be real – as indeed many of the findings of modern science confirm.

The Holy Spirit is the least 'personalized' member of the Blessed Trinity, and so it is fortunate that he is often described in these terms. From the very beginning he is described as 'wind' — the first words of the bible tell of the gales that blew over the formless wastes of creation. The image of 'breath', the breath of life that Jesus gives to the world, is obviously related closely to the same idea. The image of fire is less frequently used in this connection to describe the work of the Holy Spirit, but the Pentecost story amply makes up for this.

In the two charts which follow, the two images of wind and fire are placed side by side with a description of the work of the Holy Spirit. In this way the richness of both images should be made more obvious.

FIRE/FIRE/FIRE/FIRE/FIRE/FIRE

Fire spreads warmth to others.	The Holy Spirit brings warmth and love to people's hearts.
Fire 'welds' things together: two pieces of metal can be joined together by its power.	The Holy Spirit unites people together, when they are divided.
Fire brings light, as in a bonfire at night.	The Holy Spirit brings light to people's minds.
Fire can have a sudden and massive effect that can spread for miles – as in a forest fire.	The Holy Spirit can have a powerful effect also to the 'very ends of the world'.
Fire flickers as if it was not real, even though we know from experience that it can be powerful and strong.	The Holy Spirit may be 'invisible' but this does not mean that he is less than real. Many people have found out from their own experience how strong he is.

WIND/WIND/WIND/WIND/WIND/WIND

The wind is strong – it can blow down a house or sink a ship at sea.

The Holy Spirit is strong – he can do marvellous things.

The wind is invisible – and yet it is extraordinarily strong.

The Holy Spirit is 'invisible' – and yet he too is extraordinarily strong.

The wind cannot be 'controlled' completely – it blows 'wherever it wants'. It is stronger than human beings.

The Holy Spirit cannot be 'controlled' – the Holy Spirit 'blows wherever it wants'. It is stronger than human beings and we can be surprised to find the Holy Spirit doing good where we least expect it.

The wind can be used for a good purpose – as in a windmill which uses the power of the wind and turns it into electricity. Man must therefore learn to co-operate with the wind for he cannot simply overpower it.

The Holy Spirit gives us the power to do good, and we must therefore learn to co-operate with the Holy Spirit.

The breath we breathe is like the wind, like a breeze that blows in and out of our bodies. We breathe in the air that is all around us.

The Holy Spirit is at work both 'all around us' and 'in us'.
If we look at the world around us we will see many examples of people's goodness and kindness which the Holy Spirit 'inspires' in them.
If we look at ourselves we will find the Holy Spirit is at work 'in us' leading us to follow Christ.

The air we breathe is one of the chief *signs* of life – a person who is not breathing is very likely to be dead.

The presence of the Holy Spirit 'in us' is one of the chief signs that we are alive spiritually – if people cannot see any of the fruits of the Holy Spirit in us (i.e. peace, patience, love and joy) then they are likely to decide that we are 'spiritually dead'.

The air we breathe is also *essential* for our physical life – if a person stops breathing long enough (e.g. because he is under the water and drowning) he will simply die.

The Holy Spirit is *essential* for our spiritual life – if we refuse the help of the Holy Spirit by our sinfulness, then we can kill the spiritual life within us.

E. THE HOLY SPIRIT TODAY

1. St Paul tells us that this same Holy Spirit is given to everyone who is baptised.

The Holy Spirit helps them

to believe in Christ more strongly.

to show the love of Christ to others.

to make all God's people united and dedicated.

This Holy Spirit helps Christians in many ways, e.g. with wisdom, understanding, right judgement, courage, knowledge, reverence, wonder and awe. These virtues, often called 'the gifts of the Holy Spirit', are found in the Book of Isaiah (11 : 2). The exact words, however, are taken from the rite of confirmation itself.

If there is time available, it would be good for the candidates to work out for themselves practical examples of how each of these virtues might be put into action.

The Gifts of the Holy Spirit[12]

Wisdom: to help us to be truly wise and to follow the way of God.

Understanding: to help us to see things as God sees them.

Right judgement: to help us to recognize what is good and what is bad according to the Law of God.

Courage: to help us to follow the way of God bravely whatever the difficulties or hardships this may demand.

Knowledge: to help us to recognize the goodness and the greatness of God and to appreciate his kindness to us.

Reverence: to help us to show God the love, the honour and the respect he deserves from us.

Wonder and awe: to help us to appreciate something of the glory of God.

2. Christ said that anyone could tell a good tree or a bad tree from the kind of fruit that grew on its branches. It is also true that you can tell what *people* are like by their 'fruits'. The following virtues have often been called 'the Fruits of the Holy Spirit' because they all grow more strongly in those who allow the Holy Spirit to work in them. These virtues are to be found listed in Galatians (5: 22), and are given here in the R. S. V. Bible translation.

Once again, if there is time available, it would be good for the candidates to work out practical examples of each of these virtues in action.

The Fruits of the Holy Spirit
Love and joy
Peace and patience
Kindness and goodness
Faithfulness and gentleness and self-control

---

[12] Such a precise definition of these largely parallel virtues is bound to be arbitrary. But this list at least covers the main areas of concern intended by the words.

3. It is not difficult to give the impression that these 'gifts' and 'fruits' of the Spirit are purely individualistic virtues. But while it is true that the Holy Spirit is given for the personal development of the individual person in holiness, it is also given for the building up of the whole Body of Christ. This fact needs to be emphasised. To underline it, St Paul draws attention to another list of 'spiritual gifts' (often called 'charisms') which are even more clearly intended for the benefit of the whole community of God's people.

'There are different kinds of spiritual gifts, but the same Spirit gives them. There are different ways of serving, but the same Lord is served. There are different abilities to perform service, but the same God gives ability to everyone for their particular service. The Spirit's presence is shown in some way in each person for the good of all.

The Spirit gives one person a message full of wisdom, while to another person the same Spirit gives a message full of knowledge. One and the same Spirit gives faith to one person, while to another person he gives the power to heal. The Spirit gives one person the power to work miracles, to another the gift of speaking God's message, and to yet another the ability to tell the difference between gifts that come from the Spirit and those that do not.

It is one and the same Spirit who does all this; as he wishes, he gives a different gift to each person.'

(from I Corinthians 12 verses 4–10, 11
in the Good News Bible version)

From this text it is clear that the Spirit of God is given to people for the benefit of others, for this Spirit is a spirit of unity and cooperation uniting Christians around Christ into one single Body.[13]

[13] See also Romans 12: 4–8 for another text that underlines the fact that our differing spiritual gifts have been given to us to build up the Body of Christ. Although this text does not specifically mention the Holy Spirit by name, it is very close in intention to the text from Corinthians. It also provides yet another list of gifts or charisms which may be more immediately relevant to everyday life.

F. SUMMARY

Who is the Holy Spirit?
The Holy Spirit is 'the Gift of God'
who shares his life with all mankind.
He guides us, and he strengthens us
to help us all to follow Christ with faith and love
in the unity of his holy Church.

Here are some prayers concerning the Holy Spirit taken from
the Eucharistic Prayer of the Mass.
   God our Father,
   we thank you for counting us worthy
   to stand in your presence and serve you.
   May all of us who share in the body and blood of Christ
   be brought together in unity by the Holy Spirit.
                              (from Eucharistic Prayer II)

   God our Father,
   look with favour on your Church's offering,
   and grant that we who are nourished
   by the body and blood of Christ,
   may be filled with the Holy Spirit
   and become one body, one spirit in Christ.
                              (from Eucharistic Prayer III)

   Father, we acknowledge your greatness:
   all your actions show your wisdom and love.
   You formed man in your own likeness
   and set him over the whole world
   to serve you, his creator,
   and to rule over all creatures.
   Even when he disobeyed you and lost your friendship
   you did not abandon him to the power of death,
   but helped all men to seek and find you.
   Again and again you offered a covenant to man,
   and through the prophets taught him to hope for salvation.

Father, you so loved the world,
that in the fullness of time
you sent your only Son to be our Saviour.
He was conceived through the power of the Holy Spirit,
and born of the Virgin Mary,
a man like us in all things but sin.
To the poor he proclaimed the good news of salvation,
to prisoners, freedom,
to those in sorrow, joy.
In fulfilment of your will
he gave himself up to death;
but by rising from the dead,
he destroyed death and restored life.
And that we might live no longer for ourselves but for him,
he sent the Holy Spirit from you, Father
as his first gift to those who believe,
to complete his work on earth
and bring us the fullness of grace.

(from Eucharistic Prayer IV)

TRADITIONAL HYMNS TO THE HOLY SPIRIT
There are two traditional hymns to the Holy Spirit in Latin
and two traditional translations of them both into English:
Veni Creator Spiritus (Come Holy Ghost, Creator, Come)
Veni Sancte Spiritus (Holy Spirit, Lord of Light)
These are available in most hymnals.

There is also a translation of each of these in *New Hymns
for all Seasons* James Quinn S.J. (Geoffrey Chapman 1969).
Though these new translations are by no means modern in
style, and are set to traditional hymn tunes, they may be
found to provide a more intelligible version of the Latin
originals.

MODERN HYMNS TO THE HOLY SPIRIT
There are a remarkably large number of hymns to the Holy
Spirit written and composed in recent years, especially under
the influence of the Charismatic Movement. The following

three are all written in the 'folk' style and are readily available in many of the published collections of folk material:

God's Spirit is in my heart (the missionary power of the Spirit)

Spirit of God in the clear running waters (the Spirit and creation)

We are one in the Spirit (the Spirit and unity)

CHAPTER 5

A CHURCH OF SAINTS

At baptism the priest asks the parents of each child to renew the promises of their own baptism. This is part of the last of the questions he asks them:
'Do you believe in the holy catholic Church,
the communion of saints, the forgiveness of sins,
the resurrection of the body and life everlasting?'
The parents reply: 'I DO'.

At confirmation the bishop asks the candidates to answer the same question for themselves, and they reply 'I DO' in the same way.

A. WE KNOW AND LOVE GOD AS MEMBERS OF HIS CHURCH

God has called us to be members of his Church so that we may learn to know, love and serve him better.

At baptism our parents and our godparents promised to help us to grow up to be mature Christians; and we can learn a great deal about the love of God at home with our families.

In our catholic schools we can continue what was begun at home by learning more about the teachings of Christ. Our school is a small scale model of the world-wide 'family of God' with all its variety.

Each Sunday at Mass we join with other followers of Christ (with an even greater variety of people than we meet at school) as the 'People of God' in our own particular area, gathered together to give God the worship he deserves.

We usually 'meet' the Church at this local parish level, but, of course this is only one 'part' of the Church – the

Church in our area. Our parish belongs to a diocese which links together a hundred or more parishes in one particular part of the country. The dioceses of any one country are usually linked together through their bishops in a national 'Conference of Bishops'. All the countries of the world are united under the direction of the Bishop of Rome, the Pope.

The work of the Church can be viewed from the local and national and international level. All sorts of examples can be given of this at each level – the ones given here are merely a few of the most obvious. There are local catholic and Christian charities supporting the work of each parish and each area, e.g. in looking after the sick or the handicapped. There are national charities tackling problems nationwide, e.g. working for human rights and racial justice. There are also organisations with even wider concerns, e.g. Cafod which helps the poor and the hungry abroad and is closely involved with international development schemes.

The people involved in the work of the Church are as varied as the tasks they perform. There are priests and deacons, monks and nuns, continuing the 'work of Christ' both at home and abroad in a whole variety of ways. But quite apart from them, there are a vast number of others who devote their efforts to the work of the Church without whom the Church simply could not continue either at the local or the national or even the international level. The Church IS 'People working for Christ'.

It is important for young people to get to know their local Church, for in a sense that is where they belong. But it is also important to have some knowledge of the world-wide dimension of the Church, and to be proud of the work that is done by the Church throughout the countries of the world.

B. OUR DIOCESE, OUR BISHOP

The celebration of the sacrament of confirmation offers a good opportunity for children to find out something about their own diocese and about their bishop. The following questionnaire should be taken down in the children's work books, and completed.[14]

I

a What is the name of your bishop . . . . .
b Where does he live . . . . .
c Where was he born . . . . .
d When was he ordained priest . . . . .
e Where did he work as a priest . . . . .
f When was he ordained bishop . . . . .
g Have you ever seen the bishop . . . . .
   if so, where . . . . .
h Try and find a photograph of your bishop from a newspaper etc. and put it in your work book.

II

a What diocese does your area belong to . . . . .
b Where is the cathedral of your diocese . . . . .
c Give a list of the parishes in your area . . . . .
d Draw a simple map of your diocese, giving the main towns, etc.

A prayer from the confirmation Mass (from the bidding prayers) about the bishop:
   Let us pray for the holy Church of God,
   in union with N. our Pope, N. our Bishop and all the Bishops,
   that God, who gathers us together by the Holy Spirit,
   may help us grow in unity of faith and love
   until his Son returns in glory.

C. A CHURCH OF SAINTS

So far this brief look at the Church has considered only the Church in the world. Many children would not think of the

[14] If it should happen that a bishop other than the bishop of the local diocese is to confirm the candidates, then it would be preferable that the children find out something about the person who is to give the sacrament to them, and this questionnaire should be revised accordingly.

word 'church' having any other meaning than this. All the more reason then to draw their attention to that other dimension of the Church, namely, the Church of the saints in glory. This short section concentrates on this subject.

First it is good for them to realize that the Church includes some quite extraordinary heroes and giants, people of outstanding courage, intelligence and kindness. Sometimes young people see only the imperfections of the Church and are blinded to the powerful effect the gospel has had on the followers of Christ. They forget that the Church is called to be a Church of saints even in this world, 'perfect as our heavenly Father is perfect!'

Secondly there is the business of confirmation names. It remains customary for children to choose for themselves a new 'confirmation name' on the occasion of the celebration of this sacrament. This is no longer obligatory; in some ways it is not entirely desirable. But it remains popular, even if it does place excessive importance on a peripheral element in the rite, and detracts from the connection between confirmation and baptism. However, the rite itself leaves the option open.

If children are to choose a new name, they should choose a saint's name. Often the choice will be influenced more by the name of a friend or a celebrity, or by the 'sound' of a name, than by any religious reasons. Often a non-Christian name will be chosen, in fact. So there is a definite need for teachers to encourage their children to think about the whole thing more deeply – this set of questions might help them to do so.

WHAT IS A SAINT?

1

What is a saint?

Write an answer to this question in twenty words.

Some suggestions: the word 'saint' is sometimes used to describe all of the following – though obviously in different ways:

any member of God's family who has been baptised

any member of God's family living with him in heaven

any member of God's family whose life has been carefully investigated by the Church, and has been canonized, because they are exceptionally good and especially worthy of being imitated.

2

Name five saints who have been canonized by the Church.

Then briefly explain why the Church should want us to follow their example.

3

a) Write down your own 'Christian' name . . . . .

> (*note:* a 'Christian' name is the name of the saint after whom you were called).

b) Explain briefly what this saint was famous for . . . . .

4

a) Write down your sponsor's 'Christian' name . . . . .

b) Try and find out your sponsor's confirmation name and write this down also . . . . .

5

It is not necessary to choose another saint to be your patron saint at confirmation. You do not have to choose a new 'confirmation' name. But if you decide to do so, write down your new name, and explain briefly what your new patron saint was famous for.

NOTE: If there is sufficient time, it would be a good idea to read the story of one of the saints at this point. The lives of the Forty Martyrs can be very effective, so also the story of Father Kolbe or even a modern hero like Mother Teresa of Calcutta.

D. THE SACRAMENTS ARE ACTIONS OF CHRIST AND HIS CHURCH

The work of salvation is carried on by the Church in many different ways. God gives us particular 'privileged' occasions called sacraments when we can experience the special *power* of his love, but he clearly chooses to work in many other quite unpredictable ways as well. Something of that enormous variety of 'avenues' chosen by God is seen in the way he clearly works through all Christian churches, leading people to great heights of sanctity. Equally evidently he works through non-Christian religions, and also through non-believers, if they genuinely try to work for good and against evil.

This short section merely aims to place the seven sacraments within the framework of the saving work of the Church, as *especially privileged occasions* when we meet the Christ who died for us. Clearly the whole section could become excessively long. It is not intended to become a complete revision of all seven sacraments. To avoid this, it may be a good idea to use one of the following suggestions as a way of looking briefly at the other six sacraments, before continuing with a more thorough treatment of confirmation itself:

a) one approach would be simply to ask 'What is baptism?', 'What is the Eucharist?' etc., and to organise the resulting answers in summary form as a quick reminder of the importance of the seven sacraments.

b) an alternative approach would be to go through the various actions characteristic of each of the sacraments (e.g. the anointing with oil in the sacrament of the sick). This would be a useful preparation of the consideration of the use of 'signs' or 'actions' in the sacrament of confirmation.

c) a further alternative could be to ask how the *Church* is 'involved' in the celebration of each of the sacraments (e.g. by the presence of the priest as an official witness in the sacrament of marriage, or as the one who welcomes the sinner back to the family of God in confession), as a reminder that all the sacraments are 'sacraments of the Church'.

One of the prayers taken from the Blessing at the end of the confirmation Mass, which emphasises the work of each Christian as a member of the Church, is this:

Jesus Christ the Son of God
promised that the Spirit of truth
would be with his Church for ever:

may he bless you and give you courage
in professing the true faith.

Another prayer of blessing from the end of the confirmation
Mass, which underlines the same point:
God our Father,
complete the work you have begun
and keep the gifts of the Holy Spirit
active in the hearts of your people.
Make them ready to live his gospel
and eager to do his will.
May they never be ashamed
to proclaim to all the world Christ crucified
living and reigning for ever and ever.

Part Three

The Rite of Confirmation

CHAPTER 6

THE SACRAMENT OF CONFIRMATION (1)

NOTE 1: This section is most important for an accurate understanding of the sacrament of confirmation. It approaches this question from the standpoint of the relationship between confirmation and baptism. The teacher, or catechist, is encouraged to re-read the introductory section on the history of the sacrament (see p. 1ff) to see how closely both sacraments were related to each other in early times.

The first part of the section provides a short discussion of baptism itself. The second half attempts to distinguish baptism from confirmation. Baptism is presented as the first meeting between Christ and his disciples and confirmation as the later strengthening of the disciples through an increase of the gifts of the Holy Spirit. This is a deliberately poetic way of distinguishing these two sacraments, especially for young teenagers for whom confirmation has followed several years after baptism.

It should be obvious that this is only the beginnings of a full understanding of baptism and confirmation. Baptism is much more than simply a meeting with Christ. It is a full sharing in the life of Christ through dying and rising with him. It is a complete orientation of a person's life towards Christ, their Saviour. In a similar way confirmation is more than a strengthening of a baptised person. It is a 'perfecting' of what began at baptism – a continuation and fulfilling of the sacrament of baptism.

It may be, however, that some teachers will find this understanding of confirmation less immediately attractive than the long-standing and popular idea of 'becoming a soldier of Christ' at confirmation. And yet the history of the development of this sacrament would suggest this military image can be misleading in spite of its value, largely because it links confirmation exclusively with several ideas that rightly belong first to baptism. In practice the idea of 'becoming more like Christ' can be made equally attractive through a clear and imaginative presentation of the work of Christ as priest, prophet and king as given in the next chapter (pp. 70ff).

NOTE II: THE DISTINCTIVENESS OF THE SEVEN SACRAMENTS

In one sense all the sacraments are very similar to each other. They are all concerned with the same thing: the saving work of Christ, and our sharing in this. Their distinctiveness arises from the fact that each sacrament is concerned with a particular aspect of the saving work of Christ, or more exactly with a particular way in which we share in this.

The three 'sacraments of initiation' (i.e. baptism, confirmation and the eucharist), are even more closely related than any of the others, precisely because they are concerned with the same process of '*becoming* a Christian'. Certainly baptism and confirmation have a very similar area of reference. Their distinctness lies in the fact that baptism is the occasion when a Christian shares in the saving work of Christ *through a celebration of his death and resurrection*, while confirmation is the occasion when we do this *through a celebration of the outpouring of the Holy Spirit at Pentecost*. It could be said that we have two distinct sacraments because in historical terms there were two distinct occasions when the disciples experienced the transforming power of God – and both left a distinct and lasting impression on them.[15]

Since this is so, teachers should not be too concerned if they find themselves re-applying many of the ideas connected with baptism in relation to confirmation. But they should nevertheless at least attempt to present this material from the standpoint of the apostles who were present at that remarkable outpouring of the Holy Spirit at Pentecost.

---

[15] See pages 10–11 for a further exploration of this idea. 'Celebration' here is used in the special sense of a sacramental representation of the events of the death and resurrection of Christ as in the Mass and of the outpouring of the Holy Spirit at Pentecost in confirmation.

At baptism the priest asks the parents of each child to renew the promises of their own baptism. He asks them if they are prepared to reject sin and to live as God's children, using the following three short questions:

'Do you reject sin so as to live in the freedom of God's children?

Do you reject the glamour of evil and refuse to be mastered by sin?

Do you reject Satan, Father of sin and prince of darkness?'

To each of these questions the parents answer, 'I DO'.

At confirmation the bishop asks the candidates if they are prepared to reject sin and to live as God's children, but on this occasion he does so using one question only as follows:

'Do you reject Satan and all his works
and all his empty promises?'

The candidates reply 'I DO'.

We say 'we reject Satan' because we are ready and willing to turn away from sin in order to follow Christ more perfectly. But we also remember that sin can often be very attractive – when we do wrong, we usually do so expecting to get some enjoyment or happiness out of it. This question (and its answer) reminds us that this expectation is a kind of 'empty promise'. True happiness is only to be found in following Christ.

A. BAPTISM

At baptism we were turned away from sin
        we were brought to God our Father
        we joined the family of God, the Church
        we began to follow Christ and to believe in him.

The priest poured the water of baptism on our head, and at the same time he said

'I baptise you in the name of the Father and of the Son and of the Holy Spirit.'

He gave us new life (everything needs water to live).

He 'washed' us 'clean' from sin (the word 'baptise' comes from a Greek word meaning 'to wash clean').

This was all *done for us* at baptism.

Our parents and godparents promised that they would help us to be Christians, because they wanted us to *start* on the right path. They wanted us –

to obey God the Father,

to follow Christ,

to live as faithful members of the Church.

But once we grow up sufficiently to understand these things, it is essential that we *affirm* our baptismal promises for ourselves.

We can do this in all sorts of ways – by our prayers, and especially by our acts of faith, and by our ordinary living as faithful Christians. But there are also several *public* occasions when the Church invites us to renew our baptismal promises:

– at the baptism of other people. Parents and godparents are specifically asked to renew their own baptismal promises on these occasions, but other people can do so as well.

– each Sunday at Mass in the 'creed'. The creed is obviously much longer than the baptismal promises, but it expresses the same faith.

– most importantly of all, at Easter time, at the Holy Saturday 'Vigil' or at the Easter Sunday Masses. On this occasion the whole congregation is invited to proclaim their faith together using the exact same words as the baptismal promises.

The renewal of the baptismal promises at confirmation is therefore one further special occasion for the candidates (and indeed all the other people present at the celebration of this sacrament) to show yet again in public that they are truly 'people of faith'.

At baptism our parents and godparents say and do everything for us.

But in confirmation:

When the bishop says 'Do you believe?'

WE say 'I DO', not our parents.

When the bishop says 'BE SEALED WITH THE GIFT OF THE HOLY SPIRIT'.

WE say 'AMEN'.

At confirmation we repeat our baptismal promises in public to show that we really are 'children of God'.

to show

that we ourselves want to obey God and
                        to help other people to do the same
that we ourselves want to follow Christ and
                        to help other people to follow him
that we ourselves want to live as faithful members of his
                        Church and
                        to help other people to live in the
                        same way.

B. CONFIRMATION

At baptism we became members of God's family 'in the name of the Father and of the Son and of the Holy Spirit'. At baptism we *began* our lives as Christians. We became 'like Christ'.

The Church pictures baptism as our first meeting with Christ. At baptism we are like the first disciples of Christ who met him for the first time down by the sea in Galilee.

At confirmation we receive the 'seal of the gift of the Holy Spirit'. At confirmation we are *strengthened* as Christians and become '*more* like Christ'.

The Church pictures confirmation in terms of the 'outpouring of the Holy Spirit' at Pentecost. At confirmation we are like the followers of Christ who waited in the Upper Room for him to send down on them the Spirit of power and understanding. They were already 'friends of Christ' – they had been the followers of Christ for several years, and many of them had been working closely with Christ teaching others about the Good News and even working miracles. But now Christ was no longer visible to them, they received a new 'outpouring of the Holy Spirit' to *help them to continue* the work of Christ. Jesus did not leave them 'alone'. He kept the promise he had made to them before his death. And his 'gift' to them of the Holy Spirit gave them all the help and support they needed.

The following prayer, taken from the confirmation Mass, emphasizes this 'outpouring' of the Holy Spirit which we receive at confirmation.

My dear friends,
in baptism God our Father gave the new birth of eternal
    life
to his chosen sons and daughters.
Let us pray to the Father
that he will pour out the Holy Spirit
to strengthen his sons and daughters with his gifts
and anoint them to be more like Christ the Son of God.

Baptism and confirmation are therefore obviously very closely connected. Once upon a time they were usually given together in one ceremony. Even today, when people are baptised as adults, it is usual for the priest who is baptising them to confirm them also, even if the bishop himself cannot be present. However, if we are confirmed some time after baptism, then we have a valuable opportunity of asking ourselves if we are living up to our baptismal promises. Confirmation gives us the chance to ask the Holy Spirit to help us to become *more* like Christ, and we can be sure in this sacrament that he will give us all the help we need.

Baptism cannot be performed twice – once we are baptised, we are baptised for life, even if we are very bad catholics afterwards. In the same way once we are confirmed, we are confirmed for life, and we cannot be confirmed again. We cannot be confirmed twice. Once confirmed, always confirmed, even if we become the greatest sinners in the world afterwards. However, even if we cannot be confirmed a second time, this does not mean that we only receive the 'out-pouring' of the Holy Spirit once in a life-time. We receive the help of the Holy Spirit on many occasions during life, and especially each time we receive the sacraments.[16]

C. GROWING UP AS FOLLOWERS OF CHRIST

NOTE: Another questionnaire to be written into the work book and completed.

As already shown in the Introduction for Teachers, confirmation is *not* a sacrament of 'growing up'. It is misleading to suggest that it is. On the other hand, if this sacrament is to be delayed in the customary manner to pre-adolescence or later, then candidates should be encouraged to become aware of the spiritual growth that has (or should have) taken place in them since their baptism. It is also essential that they *respond* to the sacrament in a way that adequately reflects their age and experience.

This series of questions employs the idea of physical growth and change as a 'way in' to an investigation of less obvious changes in a person to help candidates recognize their 'growth and development as a Christian'.

[16] In the past a great deal of emphasis has been placed on this unrepeatability of confirmation. Traditional theology has always said that this sacrament, along with baptism and holy orders, had a permanent effect upon a candidate, even when there was no outward sign of this (this fact was also given official recognition at the Council of Trent 1545). This permanent effect is termed the 'character' of the sacrament.

Without wishing to question the fact of the matter, it remains true that the theology of this sacramental character is not always easy to follow. The word itself is not very helpful. The popular idea of a permanent 'mark on the soul' is positively misleading. It would seem better not to use the term at all, and to place the emphasis on the simple fact that this sacrament cannot be repeated – 'once confirmed, always confirmed'.

1. Give at least four ways in which you have changed since you first came to this school (or over the last four years, if this is longer).

    e.g. how much taller are you .....
       how much heavier .....
       any change in your hair style .....
       any change in your style of clothes .....
       do you live in the same house .....
       any other ways in which you have changed .....

Try and remember what you were like four years ago and compare this with what you are like now.

2. These outwards signs of growth and development are important, but other less obvious 'changes' (e.g. in our attitudes or in our abilities) are even more important.

Give at least four ways in which you have changed 'in yourself' over the last four years – especially in your attitudes or interests!

    e.g. have you the same friends .....
       have you improved in sport .....
       have you become interested in different sports .....
       have you become more interested or less interested in
         your work at school .....
       do you do the same things in your free time .....
         what do you do that's different ......
       do you spend your money on the same things .....
         what different things do you spend your money
         on .....
       do you treat your parents differently .....
         in what way .....
       do you treat your teachers differently .....
         in what way .....

3. Do you think there has been any change or development in yourself as a 'follower of Christ' over the last four years
.....

Try and describe this in about twenty words .....

CHAPTER 7

THE SACRAMENT OF CONFIRMATION (2)

A. CHRIST OUR LORD IS PROPHET, PRIEST AND
   KING

The notes which follow present the bare factual ideas of prophecy, priesthood and kingship with an explanation of how Christ fulfilled them and how we can follow Christ in these particular ways. Some teachers will prefer to present this material in a more colourful fashion perhaps by means of stories that illustrate the same ideas

e.g. *for prophecy:* the story of one of the Old Testament prophets such as Jeremiah, Elijah or Amos (see the attractive presentation of their stories in *Winding Quest* pp. 221 following). Or one of the prophets of today such as Mother Teresa of Calcutta.

for priesthood: the story of Cain and Abel or of Abraham and Isaac from the Old Testament, or one of the great martyr saints who offered his life as a sacrifice to God.

for kingship: the story of David or of Solomon (especially emphasising his wisdom as a judge and king), or one of the great political leaders of recent times.

If possible some practical examples should be given of how each Christian (and especially a young teenager) could fulfil his or her priestly, prophetic and kingly roles in everyday life. Since every situation is different there is little point in giving exact examples in the text, but it is essential that these ideas are made concrete and real in practical terms.

When we are baptised, we become 'like Christ', and we begin to share in his work. The work of Christ is often described under three different headings – the work of Christ the prophet, the work of Christ the priest, and the work of Christ the king. The sacrament of confirmation 'confirms' or re-affirms our sharing in the work of Christ as priest, prophet and king, and it is important to recognize what this means in practice.

CHRIST THE PROPHET[17]

When we call Christ a 'prophet', we remember that he continued and fulfilled the work of the Old Testament prophets like Isaiah, Jeremiah and Ezekiel.

Possibly many people today would link the idea of the prophet with some kind of fortune-teller, prophesying future events, but this was certainly not the main work of the prophets in bible times. Their task was to bring people back to God, their Lord and their creator, by making them more attentive to God's teaching. The prophets were people who were especially sensitive to God's voice in the world, and they had the difficult task of making other people more sensitive to the presence of God.

Christ, of course, did this better than any of the prophets before him. As the only-begotten Son of the Father, he was in a unique position to draw people back to God, and to make them more aware of God's love and mercy.

We continue that work, following in the footsteps of Christ. This is not only the work of priests and nuns, or missionaries overseas. *All* of those who have been baptised are called to become more aware of God's voice, and to draw others closer to him. We do this in many different ways. Through our prayers we *ourselves* become more alert to God's presence, and in the ordinary situations of everyday life we have many opportunities to help *others* to become closer to him.

CHRIST THE PRIEST

When we call Christ a 'priest', we remember that he offered his life on the cross to his Father in complete dedication.

This makes us remember the work of priests long ago before the time of Christ in the Old Testament, for example. Throughout history in almost every age there have been men

[17] See also page 38.

and women who have 'made offerings of thanksgiving and praise' to God on behalf of themselves and their family or tribe or nation as a sign of their love and service and worship.

Christ, of course, made the supreme offering or sacrifice of all time on the cross totally dedicating his every breath to the love and the service of his Father. And he made this offering on behalf of all mankind. In a certain way all of us also share in the love and dedication of Christ, and all of us share in his unique sacrifice or offering. We do this each day by dedicating our own lives to the service of God, and by our prayers for others. But we do it in an outstanding manner in the Mass, where we specifically ask Christ to make our own small offering a part of his own perfect sacrifice, for our own good and for the good of all his Church.

CHRIST THE KING[18]

When we call Christ a 'king', we remember that Christ will come again in glory and make his kingdom a perfect kingdom of justice, peace and truth.

We are not thinking about the trappings of kingship – Christ often rejected these during his own life-time. But we do recall that Christ taught that he came to establish a kingdom among us, a kingdom that would grow like the seeds that grow to full maturity ready for the harvest.

Christ began the work of bringing justice, truth and peace to the world. He brought healing to those who came to him for help, whether they suffered from a physical or a spiritual sickness. He brought freedom to those who followed him, freedom from the burdens of life and from the slavery of sin.

We all have a share in continuing this work of Christ. We have the task of making the kingdom of God grow to maturity. We have the task of bringing healing and liberty to the people of our own world. In every day of our lives we have innumerable opportunities to do just this.

[18] See also pages 34—35.

The Rite of Confirmation

SUMMARY

Christ the prophet
Jesus calls men to love and serve God the Father.

Throughout his life
and especially through his death and resurrection
he proclaimed the loving kindness of God the Father.

We follow in the footsteps of Christ,
for we have been called by God
to love and serve him.
Through our baptism and our confirmation
we become more like to Christ
so that we can help others to follow him.

Christ the priest
Jesus offered himself to God the Father on our behalf.

Throughout his life
and especially through his death and resurrection
he dedicated himself to God the Father
as a perfect sacrifice of love and praise.

We follow in the footsteps of Christ,
for we have been called by God
to offer him everything that is good in our lives.
Through our baptism and our confirmation
we become more like to Christ
so that we can share in his perfect sacrifice.

Christ the king
Jesus is the king of the universe.

Throughout his life
and especially through his death and resurrection
he established the Kingdom of God
of justice, peace and truth and love.

We follow in the footsteps of Christ,

72

for we have been called by God
to make his kingdom grow on earth.
Through our baptism and our confirmation
we become more like to Christ
so that we can help to build the kingdom
   of justice, peace, and truth and love.

B. SIGNS AND SYMBOLS

The sacrament of confirmation employs several signs and symbols to draw attention to our sharing in the work of Christ, the prophet, priest and king. The anointing or 'sealing' of each candidate with the sign of the cross in chrism, the imposition of hands by the bishop and his priests, and the sign of peace given to each of the candidates all emphasise their involvement in the saving work of Christ. The next three sections consider each of these signs and symbols in more detail.

THE OIL OF CHRISM AND THE ANOINTING OF EACH CANDIDATE

NOTE: The early Church referred to the giving of the Holy Spirit as a 'pouring out' of the Spirit. This image of 'pouring out' possibly arose from Old Testament usage, in which the generous pouring of perfumed oil on a person's head symbolized the blessing of God and the giving of a spirit of power and ministry.

But the early Church also recognized that the Holy Spirit could be given to a person through 'the imposition of hands'. A detailed account of this happening is given in Acts 19: 1–6, where St Paul meets some of John the Baptist's disciples, and 'placed his hands on them so that the Holy Spirit might come down on them'.

The early Church obviously did not consider either one of these was the more correct or more effective way of inviting the Holy Spirit to bless a person. The idea probably never entered her consciousness, for she was only too aware that the Spirit could 'blow wherever he willed'. Later generations of Christians, however, have argued over the relative importance of each of these gestures. The modern Church has therefore incorporated both the anointing and the imposition of hands within the present ceremony, even though in practice she places greater importance on anointing. In many ways both actions symbolise the same thing. (See also pp. 76-7.)

What connection has oil with the following?
Vaseline .....
    What is it used for ......
Athletes .....
    What it is used for .....
Lamps .....
    What is it used for .....
Fires .....
    What is it used for .....
Machines (e.g. cars) .....
    What is it used for .....

Oil is important in connection with each of these in a slightly different way.
    a) Vaseline is an oil-based salve – for healing.
    b) Athletes used to use oil as an embrocation in ancient times – to make their limbs supple and strong.
    c) Lamps sometimes use oil as a fuel – for lighting.
    d) Fires sometimes use oil as a fuel – for heating.
    e) Machines sometimes use oil as a fuel – for power.

In the sacrament of confirmation we receive the Gift of the Holy Spirit to help us to continue the work of Christ.
We receive:
    The health and strength of the Holy Spirit.
    The light (and understanding) of the Holy Spirit.
    The warmth (and the love) of the Holy Spirit.
    The power (the 'driving force') of the Holy Spirit.

King David was 'anointed' with' oil, before he became King of Israel. The anointing was a sign of his kingly power and of the strength that God was giving to him. The kings and queens of England continue to be 'anointed' at their coronation in the same way.

74

Priests are 'anointed' with oil at their ordination as a sign that God has chosen them for his service. Bishops also are 'anointed' at their espiscopal ordination.

In all of these cases (the anointing of kings and the anointing of priests and bishops) the oil that is used is the oil of chrism, a particularly rich oil that is made up of olive oil and sweet smelling balsam.

Presumably the richness of the oil is intended to be itself a symbol of the richness of the blessing that it signifies. It is this same oil of chrism that is used in the sacrament of confirmation. And the attractive smell of the balsam reminds us that the Christian life is something good and attractive. We are, in a manner of speaking, 'lucky' to be called by Christ, to be his followers.

The oil of chrism that we use in confirmation is specially consecrated each year in a Mass in the cathedral of the diocese on Holy Thursday morning. It is consecrated like this in Holy Week because Holy Week is the time when we especially remember the death and resurrection of Christ and this oil is intended to make us more like the Christ who died for us.[19]

THE 'SEAL' OF THE HOLY SPIRIT

As the bishop 'anoints' each candidate with chrism, he says the following words

'Be sealed with the Gift of the Holy Spirit'.

Usually the word 'seal' suggests a piece of wax or lead marked with some kind of stamp, and attached to a document as a sign and guarantee of the authenticity of the document.

If a person has the 'seal' of the Holy Spirit given to them,

[19] It would be a good idea for the school chaplain or some other priest to let the candidates for confirmation see a container of the sacred chrism before the ceremony. If possible, it would be desirable to use one of the large ampullae for this purpose: most deaneries have a set of three of these, one for each of the sacred oils. The usual little oil stocks may be convenient for general use, but they give children hardly any idea of the importance which the Church places on the sacred chrism.

this is also a kind of sign and guarantee that this person is a genuine follower of Christ. If a person is not a faithful follower of Christ, and yet is still 'sealed' with the 'gift of the Holy Spirit', then that person is not 'authentic', he is a kind of fraud or cheat. In fact, to be confirmed without having any intention to live the Christian life is simply dishonest.

THE SIGN OF THE CROSS

When the bishop 'seals' each candidate with holy chrism, he does so by making the sign of the cross in oil on the forehead of each of those to be confirmed, as a reminder to them of the death of Christ on the cross.

Although we use the sign of the cross very frequently, e.g. at the beginning and the end of our prayers, it can easily become a careless, even a meaningless, gesture. We can forget that the action or prayer we are engaged in is performed *in God's name* and *for his sake*. The cross is the sign of the dedication of Christ, who was not afraid even to die on the cross for us. The bishop marks us with the sign of the cross in chrism at confirmation to remind us that we are promising to become more like Christ in our own lives.

THE IMPOSITION OF HANDS

NOTE: The 'Imposition of hands' is one of those actions taken over by the early Church from Israelite usage. Clearly the first Christians did not feel it required any explanation – it was an obvious, traditional gesture. Today the situation is somewhat different, for though the Church is increasingly returning to her former practice, and using the imposition of hands in many of her rites, the sign value of the gesture has not yet become self-explanatory.

Possibly the origin of this action lies in the simple and direct commanding gesture of a leader over his subjects – something which is still recognizable in the action of a teacher over junior children as he selects a certain number of them for a particular job, or when dividing them into teams ('I'll have you, you and you!' – at the same time physically moving them to one side). The physical contact of a person's hand on another is undoubtedly a very ancient sign of the power of one person over another.

At a deeper level, there is something even more subtle in this kind of physical contact. As the continued use of the hand-shake proves, physical contact almost seems essential to the effective communication of elusive things like friendship and gladness. Under certain circumstances, a warm handshake can indeed be more than merely a 'sign' of friendship, it becomes a kind of 'giving' of friendship: the one receiving the gesture almost seems to 'receive' something from the other 'in' the handshake itself. It is not hard to see an extension of the same idea inherent in the action of holy men of long ago, who 'gave' something of their own 'power' to their disciples through the imposition of hands upon the head of their pupils.

To a certain extent this gesture also expresses a kind of welcome to the candidate – especially as given in confirmation in conjunction with the sign of peace. Although the primary significance of the imposition of hands is one of giving a share in the work of Christ through the power of the Holy Spirit, it is nearly always employed in situations which also emphasise the element of incorporating (or re-incorporating) a candidate into the active Christian community (see the rite of penance and the anointing of the sick, which both use the imposition of hands for this purpose). It is therefore not surprising that this gesture should take on this secondary significance in confirmation, i.e. of *welcoming* a candidate to share in an increase of the life of the Spirit which he first received at baptism.

A brief examination of ideas such as these can help make this particular gesture in the rite of confirmation a great deal more meaningful.

At confirmation, just before he anoints each candidate, the bishop (and all the other priests who are assisting him,) extend their hands over the people to be confirmed. While they do so, the bishop says the following prayer:

All powerful God, Father of our Lord Jesus Christ,
by water and the Holy Spirit

you freed your sons and daughters from sin
and gave them new life.
Send your Holy Spirit upon them
to be their Helper and Guide.
Give them the spirit of wisdom and understanding,
the spirit of right judgement and courage,
the spirit of knowledge and reverence.
Fill them with the spirit of wonder and awe in your
presence.
We ask this through Christ our Lord.

Then, as he anoints each candidate, the bishop performs an individual 'imposition of hands' by making the sign of the cross on the forehead in chrism.

NOTE: This individual imposition of hands is not performed as a distinct or separate gesture. The action of touching the head with the thumb as the bishop makes the sign of the cross in chrism is itself said to be a kind of imposition of hand(s) – though in fact this may well be less than obvious. As the introduction to the rite of confirmation specifically states, the essence of the sacrament is as follows: 'the sacrament of confirmation is conferred through an anointing with chrism on the forehead *which is done by the laying on of the hand* and through the words 'be sealed with the Gift of the Holy Spirit'.

Some writers have therefore recommended the use of a completely distinct individual imposition of hands in silence immediately before the anointing in order to make the sign value of this action clearer. Although this could be said to duplicate the earlier communal imposition of hands, at least it restores the effective sign value of the gesture. (In the individual form of the sacrament, e.g. as given in danger of death, this communal imposition of hands of necessity becomes an individual action by which the bishop or priest places his hand on the candidate's head while saying the prayer 'All powerful God . . .' This is much more telling.)

In the early Church the 'imposition of hands' was used

very frequently, and we often hear about it especially in the Acts of the Apostles. It was often used as a sign of the Church's power to bless and to strengthen her members, and as a sign of forgiveness.

Today this gesture is less familiar. But one occasion of its use is at least fairly noticeable, namely at Mass when the celebrant stretches his hands over the offerings of bread and wine and prays that the Holy Spirit may bless them and make them holy.

In similar fashion, the bishop at confirmation prays that the candidates for this sacrament may become holy, and that they too may receive the blessing of the Holy Spirit of wisdom and truth.

THE IMPOSITION OF HANDS ON ST PAUL
AND THE BEGINNING OF HIS LIFE AS A MISSIONARY
The story of the imposition of hands on Saul/Paul now follows as an example of the use of the imposition of hands in the early Church.

NOTE: In this story the action of the imposition of hands is performed *before* the baptism of Saul, and indeed he appears to have 'received the Holy Spirit' before he was baptised with water. Many children would probably never notice this and it hardly needs to be emphasised. But if questions should be asked, the only answer that can be given is that the Apostolic Church was not very concerned about making rules about this kind of thing. She was much more concerned to look out for 'signs' of the work and presence of the Holy Spirit *wherever* he chose to work – and however unexpectedly!

In the story of the conversion of St Paul, we hear how 'Saul' is struck down from his horse and is led away 'blindly' to recover in a house in Damascus. While he is there, he prays for God's help, and a man called Ananias is sent by God to bless him.

'When Ananias found Saul,
he was saying his prayers
   in a house in Straight Street.
So he went in and blessed him
   with his hands outstretched over Saul.
"Brother Saul", he said,
"Jesus has sent me to help you.
Receive the Holy Spirit."
And at once Saul could see again;
   and he asked to be baptised immediately.'
                (from Acts 9: 17 ff.
                from A. J. McCallen, *Listen!*)

After his baptism, Paul became a missionary for Christ, going all over the world taking the message of Christ to all kinds of people. Indeed St Paul is a wonderful example of the way we can follow the example of Christ as prophet, priest and king.

THE SIGN OF PEACE

NOTE: Increasingly the 'sign of peace' is being given at least at children's Masses, even if it is still not generally accepted in adult liturgies. Most of the candidates should therefore have some idea of what is intended by the 'sign of peace' which is given by the bishop after the anointing at confirmation. However, though they use the familiar words 'peace be with you', many bishops retain the old gesture of a gentle pat on the cheek in place of the more common hand shake, which may not be immediately self-evident to children as meaning the same thing. This probably requires explanation, for many people will naturally still think of the more traditional gesture as a 'cuff' on the cheek, a kind of test of strength, rather than as a sign of endearment.

After the anointing with chrism at confirmation, the bishop says to each person 'peace be with you' and gives them a sign of peace.

Each candidate then says in a clear voice 'And also with you.'

The bishop is the person who is 'at the centre' of the whole diocese. He is the one who keeps the diocese faithful to Christ and united within itself. He is the local 'head' of the 'body' of the Church.

At confirmation, he reminds each candidate that he is their friend, and also that he is their guide and teacher.

He asks them therefore to be faithful members of the Church.

He asks them to live in peace and gentleness and consideration with the other members of the Church.

He prays that they may help make the Church a good example to the rest of the world, so that 'inspired by the good lives of Christians', all mankind may one day be joined together in the peace and joy of God's kingdom.

The following words are taken from one of the bidding prayers of the confirmation Mass.

Let us pray to the Lord for all men
of every race and nation,
that they may acknowledge the one God as Father,
and in the bond of common brotherhood
seek his kingdom
which is peace and joy in the Holy Spirit.

CHAPTER 8

THE CONFIRMATION MASS

The previous pages have considered in detail the words and actions connected with the sacrament of confirmation, and have looked at many of the other prayers of the confirmation Mass. All that remains is to run through the words and actions of the ceremony in the order in which they will occur on the confirmation day itself (see Appendix II, pp. 102ff).

The responses said by the candidates are short in length and few in number. It should not be too difficult therefore to practise them with each child so that he or she can say them clearly, distinctly and with confidence.

The Introduction to the Rite of Confirmation states that ordinarily confirmation should take place within Mass in order to express clearly the fundamental connection of this sacrament with the entirety of Christian initiation. The latter reaches its culmination in the communion of the body and blood of Christ. The newly confirmed should therefore participate in the eucharist which completes their Christian initiation (see section 13). Attention should be paid to the festive and solemn character of the liturgical service, and its significance for the local Church. The whole people of God represented by the families and friends of the candidates and by members of the local community, should be invited to take part in the celebration, and will express its faith in the fruits of the Holy Spirit (see section 4).

Obviously it is highly desirable for those who are to be confirmed to go to communion within the confirmation Mass. It also is very desirable for them to go to the sacrament of penance in preparation for their confirmation.

The occasion of a confirmation could be a suitable opportunity for the bishop to make use of (or even to introduce) one of the new Eucharistic Prayers for children. Though supposedly intended for very young children, they are sufficiently adult in their style to be used with much older age groups. The second of these includes many references to the work of the Holy Spirit. The third prayer allows for a variable section before the consecration, and it would not be difficult to commission a new 'part' on the work of the Holy Spirit for inclusion at this point (see the Introduction to Eucharistic Prayers for Children, para 23).

It is a good idea for some of those being confirmed to bring the bread and the wine for the Mass to the altar in an offertory procession. Similarly it would be attractive if some of them also read the Bidding Prayers. It is also very fitting for the candidates to receive holy communion under both kinds on this occasion. Although a large number of candidates along with a good-sized congregation may appear to preclude this, it is something of sufficient importance to merit the effort and organization required.

The bishop and any priests who are present (the rite presumes they will generally be concelebrating with him), usually wear white or red vestments for the confirmation Mass. Red, of course, is the colour of the 'fire' of the Holy Spirit. Perhaps it could also be explained that it is the colour of martyrs as well – for they were so 'filled with the Holy Spirit' that they were prepared even to die for their Lord, Jesus Christ.

The people present at the confirmation Mass
The bishop
The priests of the parish
The people to be confirmed
The sponsors
Parents and friends
Members of the parish

What does the bishop do?
He will extend his hands over all those to be confirmed and
   pray for them.

He will sign you with the cross in chrism, and say:
    '(Peter or Mary etc.) be sealed with the Gift of the Holy
      Spirit.'
He will give you the 'sign of peace', and say:
    'Peace be with you.'

What do you do?
You will take a full part in the Mass, especially by listening to
    what is said and by joining in the hymns and the
    responses.
You will renew your baptismal promises along with the other
    candidates,
    and when the bishop says 'Do you believe . . . . ?'
    you will say 'I DO' clearly and distinctly.
You will go forward with your sponsor to receive the sign of
    the cross in chrism on your forehead.
When the bishop says 'Be sealed with the Gift of the Holy
    Spirit' you will reply 'AMEN'.
When the bishop gives you the sign of peace and says 'Peace
    be with you' you will reply 'AND ALSO WITH YOU'.

CONFIRMATION CARDS
It is customary for each candidate to have a confirmation
card. Usually this is issued by the local school or parish
through which the confirmations are being organized. This
card contains those details required by the bishop from the
candidate for confirmation, and it is normally handed to the
bishop or an assistant priest by the candidate himself or his
sponsor as they go up for the anointing. The following
example includes all that is ordinarily required.

After the ceremony it is important that this card is given to
the senior priest of the place of confirmation or someone
deputed by him so that the various details of each candidate
can be entered in the baptismal register of his or her place of
baptism and in the confirmation register of the place of
confirmation.

Full name   Philip Smith
Parish   St Stephen's, Hull
place of baptism   St Mary's, Hull
date of baptism   1.v.1963
place of confirmation   Sacred Heart, Hull
date of confirmation   1.vi.1977
confirmation sponsor   Mrs R. Wilson
Baptismal name (or confirmation name if required)
  PHILIP

The Decree, Apostolic Constitution and General Introduction to the Rite of Confirmation

SACRED CONGREGATION FOR DIVINE WORSHIP

Prot. n. 800/71

DECREE

In the sacrament of confirmation the apostles and the bishops who are their successors have handed on to the baptised the special gift of the Holy Spirit, promised by Christ the Lord and poured out upon the apostles at Pentecost. With this the initiation in the Christian life is completed so that believers are strengthened by power from heaven, made true witnesses of Christ in word and deed, and bound more closely to the Church.

To make 'the intimate connection of this sacrament with the whole of Christian initiation' clearer, the Second Vatican Council decreed that the rite of confirmation should be revised.

Now that this work has been completed and approved by Pope Paul VI in the apostolic constitution *Divinae consortium naturae* of August 15, 1971, the Congregation for Divine Worship has published the new Rite of Confirmation. It is to replace the rite now in use in the Roman Pontifical and Ritual. The Congregation declares the present edition to be the typical edition.

Anything to the contrary notwithstanding.

From the office of the Congregation for Divine Worship, August 22, 1971.

Annibale Bugnini   Arturo Cardinal Tabera
Secretary   Prefect

APOSTOLIC CONSTITUTION ON
THE SACRAMENT OF CONFIRMATION

PAUL, BISHOP

Servant of the Servants of God

For an Everlasting Memorial

THE REFORM OF THE RITE[20]

The sharing in the divine nature which is granted to men through the grace of Christ has a certain likeness to the origin, development, and nourishing of natural life. The faithful are born anew by baptism, strengthened by the sacrament of confirmation, and finally are sustained by the food of eternal life in the eucharist. By means of these sacraments of Christian initiation, they thus receive in increasing measure the treasures of divine life and advance towards the perfection of charity. It has rightly been written: 'The body is washed, that the soul may be cleansed; the body is anointed, that the soul may be consecrated; the body is signed, that the soul too may be fortified; the body is overshadowed by the laying on of hands, that the soul too may be enlightened by the Spirit; the body is fed on the body and blood of Christ, that the soul too should be nourished by God.'

Conscious of its pastoral purpose, the Second Vatican Ecumenical Council devoted special attention to these sacraments of initiation. It prescribed that the rites should be suitably revised in order to make them more suited to the understanding of the faithful. Since the *Rite for the Baptism of Children*, revised at the mandate of that General Council and published at our command, is already in use, it is now fitting to publish the rite of confirmation, in order to show the unity of Christian initiation in its true light.

In fact, careful attention and application have been devoted in these last years to the task of revising the manner of celebrating this sacrament. The aim of this work has been that 'the intimate connection which this sacrament has with

[20] Headings in the Apostolic Constitution have been added by the author.

the whole of Christian initiation should be more lucidly set forth.' The link between confirmation and the other sacraments of initiation is shown forth more clearly not only by closer association of these sacraments but also by the rite and words by which confirmation is conferred. This is done so that the rite and words of this sacrament may 'express more clearly the holy things which they signify. The Christian people, so far as possible, should be able to understand them with ease and take full and active part in the celebration as a community.'

For that purpose, it has been our wish to include in this revision what concerns the very essence of the rite of confirmation, through which the faithful receive the Holy Spirit as a Gift.

THE NEW TESTAMENT

The New Testament shows how the Holy Spirit assisted Christ in fulfilling his messianic mission. On receiving the baptism of John, Jesus saw the Spirit descending on him (see Mark 1: 10) and remaining with him (see John 1: 32). He was impelled by the Spirit to undertake his public ministry as the Messiah, relying on the Spirit's presence and assistance. Teaching the people of Nazareth, he shows by what he said that the words of Isaiah, 'The Spirit of the Lord is upon me', referred to himself (see Luke 4: 17–21).

He later promised his disciples that the Holy Spirit would help them also to bear fearless witness to their faith even before persecutors (see Luke 12: 12). The day before he suffered, he assured his apostles that he would send the Spirit of truth from his Father (see John 15: 26) to stay with them 'for ever' (John 14: 16) and help them to be his witness (see John 15: 26). Finally, after his resurrection, Christ promised the coming descent of the Holy Spirit: 'You will receive power when the Holy Spirit comes down on you; then you are to be my witnesses' (Acts 1: 8; see Luke 24: 49).

And in fact, on the day of the feast of Pentecost, the Holy Spirit came down in an extraordinary way on the Apostles as they were gathered together with Mary the mother of Jesus and the group of disciples. They were so 'filled with' the Holy Spirit (Acts 2: 4) that by divine inspiration they began to proclaim 'the mighty works of God.' Peter regarded the Spirit who had thus come down upon the Apostles as the gift of the messianic age (see Acts 2: 17–18). Those who believed the Apostles' preaching were then baptised and they too received 'the gift of the Holy Spirit' (Acts 2: 38). From that time on the apostles, in fulfillment of Christ's wish, imparted the gift of the Spirit to the newly baptised by the laying on of hands to complete the grace of baptism. Hence it is that the Letter to the Hebrews lists among the first elements of Christian instruction the teaching about baptism and the laying on of hands (Hebrews 6: 2). This laying on of hands is rightly recognized by Catholic tradition as the beginning of the sacrament of confirmation, which in a certain way perpetuates the grace of Pentecost in the Church.

THE SPECIFIC IMPORTANCE OF CONFIRMATION

This makes clear the specific importance of confirmation for sacramental initiation by which the faithful 'as members of the living Christ are incorporated into him and made like him through baptism and through confirmation and the eucharist'. In baptism, the newly baptised receive forgiveness of sins, adoption as sons of God, and the character of Christ, by which they are made members of the Church and for the first time become sharers in the priesthood of their Saviour (see I Peter 2: 5, 9). Through the sacrament of confirmation, those who have been born anew in baptism receive the inexpressible Gift, the Holy Spirit himself, by which 'they are endowed...with special strength.' Moreover, having received the character of this sacrament, they are 'bound more intimately to the Church' and 'they are more strictly obliged to spread and defend the faith both by word and by deed as true witnesses of Christ.' Finally, confirmation is so closely linked with the holy eucharist that the faithful, after being signed by holy baptism and confirmation, are incorporated fully into the body of Christ by participation in the eucharist.

THE ANOINTING AND THE LAYING ON OF HANDS

From ancient times the conferring of the gift of the Holy
Spirit has been carried out in the Church with various rites.
These rites underwent many changes in the East and the
West, while always keeping the significance of a conferring
of the Holy Spirit.

In many Eastern rites, it seems that from early times a rite
of anointing, not then clearly distinguished from baptism,
prevailed for the conferring of the Holy Spirit. That rite
continues in use today in the greater part of the churches of
the East.

In the West there are very ancient witnesses concerning the
part of Christian initiation which was later distinctly
recognized as the sacrament of confirmation. After the
baptismal washing and before the eucharistic meal, the
performance of many rites is indicated, such as anointing, the
laying on of the hand and consignation. These are contained
both in liturgical documents and in many testimonies of the
Fathers. In the course of the centuries, problems and doubts
arose as to what belonged with certainty to the essence of the
rite of confirmation. It is fitting to mention at least some of
the elements which, from the thirteenth century onwards, in
the ecumenical councils and in the documents of the popes,
cast light on the importance of anointing while at the same
time not allowing the laying on of hands to be obscured.

Our predecessor Innocent III wrote: 'By the anointing of
the forehead the laying on of the hand is designated, which is
otherwise called confirmation, since through it the Holy
Spirit is given for growth and strength.' Another of our
predecessors, Innocent IV, recalls that the Apostles conferred
the Holy Spirit 'through the laying on of the hand, which
confirmation or the anointing of the forehead represents.'
In the profession of faith of Emperor Michael Palaeologus,
which was read at the Second Council of Lyons, mention is
made of the sacrament of confirmation, which 'bishops confer

by the laying on of the hands, anointing with chrism those who have been baptised.' The Decree for the Armenians, issued by the Council of Florence, declares that the 'matter' of the sacrament of confirmation is 'chrism made of olive oil ...and balsam,' and, quoting the words of the Acts of the Apostles concerning Peter and John, who gave the Holy Spirit through the laying on of hands (see Acts 8: 17), it adds: 'in place of that laying on of the hand, in the Church confirmation is given.' The Council of Trent, though it had no intention of defining the essential rite of confirmation, only designated it with the name of the holy chrism of confirmation. Benedict XIV made this declaration: 'Therefore let this be said, which is beyond dispute: in the Latin Church the sacrament of confirmation is conferred by using sacred chrism or olive oil, mixed with balsam and blessed by the bishop, and by tracing the sign of the cross by the minister of the sacrament on the forehead of the recipient, while the same minister pronounces the words of the form.'

Many theologians, taking account of these declarations and traditions, maintained that for valid administration of confirmation there was required only anointing with chrism, done by placing the hand on the forehead. In spite of this, however, in the rites of the Latin Church a laying of hands upon those to be confirmed was always prescribed before the anointing.

THE FORM OF THE RITE

With regard to the words of the rite by which the Holy Spirit is given, it should be noted that, already in the primitive Church, Peter and John, in order to complete the initiation of those baptised in Samaria, prayed for them to receive the Holy Spirit and then laid hands on them (see Acts 8: 15–17). In the East, in the fourth and fifth centuries, there appear in the rite of anointing the first indications of the words 'signaculum doni Spiritus Sancti.' These words were quickly accepted by the Church of Constantinople and are still used by the Churches of the Byzantine rite.

In the West, however, the words of this rite, which completed baptism, were not defined until the twelfth and thirteenth centuries. But in the twelfth century Roman Pontifical the formula which later became the common one first occurs: 'I sign you with the sign of the cross and confirm you with the chrism of salvation. In the name of the Father and of the Son and of the Holy Spirit.'

From what we have recalled, it is clear that in the administration of confirmation in the East and the West, though in different ways, the most important place was occupied by the anointing, which in a certain way represents the apostolic laying on of hands. Since this anointing with chrism well represents the spiritual anointing of the Holy Spirit, who is given to the faithful, we intend to confirm its existence and importance.

As regards the words which are pronounced in confirmation, we have examined with due consideration the dignity of the venerable formula used in the Latin Church, but we judge preferable the very ancient formula belonging to the Byzantine rite, by which the Gift of the Holy Spirit himself is expressed and the outpouring of the Spirit which took place on the day of Pentecost is recalled (see Acts 2: 1-4, 38). We therefore adopt this formula, rendering it almost word for word.

Therefore, in order that the revision of the rite of confirmation may fittingly embrace also the essence of the sacramental rite, by our supreme apostolic authority we decree and lay down that in the Latin Church the following should be observed for the future:

The Sacrament of Confirmation is conferred through the anointing with chrism on the forehead, which is done by the laying on of the hand, and through the words: 'Accipe Signaculum Doni Spiritus Sancti.'

Although the laying of hands on the candidates, which is done with the prescribed prayer before the anointing, does not belong to the essence of the sacramental rite, it is nevertheless to be held in high esteem, in that it contributes to the integral perfection of that rite and to a clearer understanding of the sacrament. It is evident that this preceding laying on of hands differs from the laying on of the hand by which the anointing is done on the forehead.

CONCLUSION

Having established and declared all these elements concerning the essential rite of the sacrament of confirmation, we also approve by our apostolic authority the order for the same sacrament, which has been revised by the Congregation for Divine Worship, after consultation with the Congregations for the Doctrine of the Faith, for the Discipline of the Sacraments, and for the Evangelization of Peoples as regards the matters which are within their competence. The Latin edition of the order containing the new form will come into force as soon as it is published; the editions in the vernacular languages, prepared by the episcopal conferences and confirmed by the Apostolic See, will come into force on the dates to be laid down by the individual conferences. The old order may be used until the end of the year 1972. From January 1, 1973, however, only the new order is to be used by those concerned.

We intend that everything that we have laid down and prescribed should be firm and effective in the Latin Church, notwithstanding, where relevant, the apostolic constitutions and ordinances issued by our predecessors, and other prescriptions, even if worthy of special mention.

Given in Rome, at Saint Peter's, on the fifteenth day of August, the Solemnity of the Assumption of the Blessed Virgin Mary, in the year 1971, the ninth of our pontificate.

PAUL PP. VI

GENERAL INTRODUCTION

I. DIGNITY OF CONFIRMATION

1. Those who have been baptised continue on the path of

Christian initiation through the sacrament of confirmation. In this sacrament they receive the Holy Spirit, whom the Lord sent upon the apostles at Pentecost.

2. The giving of the Holy Spirit conforms believers more perfectly to Christ and strengthens them so that they may bear witness to Christ for the building up of his body in faith and love. They are so marked with the character or seal of the Lord that the sacrament of confirmation cannot be repeated.

II. OFFICES AND MINISTRIES IN THE CELEBRATION
OF CONFIRMATION

3. It is the responsibility of the people of God to prepare the baptised for confirmation. It is the responsibility of the pastors to see that all the baptised come to the fullness of Christian initiation and are carefully prepared for confirmation.

Adult catechumens, who are to be confirmed immediately after baptism, have the help of the Christian community and, in particular, the formation which is given to them during the catechumenate, catechesis, and common liturgical celebrations. Catechists, sponsors, and members of the local church have a part in the catechumenate. The steps of the catechumenate will be appropriately adapted to those who, baptised in infancy, are confirmed only as adults.

The initiation of children into the sacramental life is for the most part the responsibility and concern of Christian parents. They are to form and gradually develop a spirit of faith in the children and, with the help of catechetical institutions, prepare them for the fruitful reception of the sacraments of confirmation and the eucharist. This responsibility of the parents is also shown by their active participation in the celebration of the sacraments.

4. Attention should be paid to the festive and solemn character of the liturgical service, and its significance for the local church, especially if all the candidates are assembled for a common celebration. The whole people of God, repre-

sented by the families and friends of the candidates and by members of the local community, will be invited to take part in the celebration and will express its faith in the fruits of the Holy Spirit.

5. Ordinarily there should be a sponsor for each of those to be confirmed. The sponsor brings the candidate to receive the sacrament, presents him to the minister for the anointing, and will later help him to fulfil his baptismal promises faithfully under the influence of the Holy Spirit.

In view of contemporary pastoral circumstances, it is desirable that the godparent at baptism, if present, also be the sponsor at confirmation; canon 796, no. 1, is abrogated. This change expresses more clearly the relationship between baptism and confirmation and also makes the function and responsibility of the sponsor more effective.

Nonetheless the choice of a special sponsor for confirmation is not excluded. Even the parents themselves may present their children for confirmation. It is for the local Ordinary to determine diocesan practice after considering local circumstances.

6. Pastors will see that the sponsor, chosen by the candidate or his family, is spiritually qualified for the office and satisfies these requirements:
   a) that he be sufficiently mature for this responsibility;
   b) that he belong to the Catholic Church and have been initiated in the three sacraments of baptism, confirmation, and the eucharist;
   c) that he be not prohibited by law from exercising the office of sponsor.

7. The original minister of confirmation is the bishop. Ordinarily the sacrament is administered by the bishop so that there will be a more evident relationship to the first pouring forth of the Holy Spirit on Pentecost. After the apostles were filled with the Holy Spirit, they themselves gave the Spirit to the faithful through the laying on of their hands. Thus the reception of the Spirit through the ministry of the bishop shows the close bond which joins the confirmed to the

Church and the mandate to be witnesses of Christ among men.

In addition to the bishop, the law gives the faculty to confirm to the following:

a) apostolic administrators who are not bishops, prelates or abbots *nullius*, vicars and prefects apostolic, vicars capitular, within the limits of their territory and while they hold office;

b) priests who, in virtue of an office which they lawfully hold, baptize an adult or a child old enough for catechesis or receive a validly baptised adult into full communion with the Church;

c) in danger of death, provided the bishop is not easily available or is lawfully impeded: pastors and parochial vicars; in their absence, their parochial associates; priests who are in charge of special parishes lawfully established; administrators; substitutes; and assistants; in the absence of all of the preceding, any priest who is not subject to censure or canonical penalty.

8. In case of true necessity and special reason, for example, the large number of persons to be confirmed, the minister of confirmation mentioned in no. 7 or the special minister designated by indult of the Apostolic See or by law may associate other priests with himself in the administration of this sacrament.

It is required that these priests:

a) have a particular function or office in the diocese, namely, vicars general, episcopal vicars or delegates, district or regional vicars, or those who by mandate of the Ordinary hold equivalent offices; or

b) be the pastors of the places where confirmation is conferred, pastors of the places where the candidates belong, or priests who have had a special part in the catechetical preparation of the candidates.

III. CELEBRATION OF THE SACRAMENT

9. The sacrament of confirmation is conferred through the anointing with chrism on the forehead, which is done by the

laying on of the hand, and through the words: *Be sealed with the Gift of the Holy Spirit.*

Even though the laying of hands on the candidates with the prayer *All-powerful God* does not pertain to the valid giving of the sacrament, it is to be strongly emphasized for the integrity of the rite and the fuller understanding of the sacrament.

Priests who are sometimes associated with the principal minister in giving the sacrament join him in laying their hands on all the candidates together, but they do not say the prayer.

The whole rite has a twofold meaning. The laying of hands on the candidates by the bishop and the concelebrating priests is the biblical gesture by which the giving of the Holy Spirit is invoked. This is well adapted to the understanding of the Christian people. The anointing with chrism and the accompanying words express clearly the effects of the giving of the Holy Spirit. Signed with the perfumed oil, the baptised person receives the indelible character, the seal of the Lord, together with the gift of the Spirit, which conforms him more closely to Christ and gives him the grace of spreading the Lord's presence among men.

10. The chrism is consecrated by the bishop in the Mass which is ordinarily celebrated on Holy Thursday for this purpose.

11. Adult catechumens and children who are baptised at an age when they are old enough for catechesis should ordinarily be admitted to confirmation and the eucharist at the same time they receive baptism. If this is impossible, they should receive confirmation in a common celebration (see no. 4). Similarly, adults who were baptised in infancy should, after suitable preparation, receive confirmation and the eucharist in a common celebration.

With regard to children, in the Latin Church the administration of confirmation is generally postponed until about the seventh year. For pastoral reasons, however, especially to strengthen the faithful in complete obedience to Christ the

Lord and in loyal testimony to him, episcopal conferences may choose an age which seems more appropriate, so that the sacrament is given at a more mature age after appropriate formation.

In this case the necessary precautions should be taken so that children will be confirmed at the proper time, even before the use of reason, when there is danger of death or other serious difficulty. They should not be deprived of the benefit of this sacrament.

12. One must be baptised to receive the sacrament of confirmation. In addition, if the baptized person has the use of reason, it is required that he be in a state of grace, properly instructed, and able to renew his baptismal promises.

It is the responsibility of the episcopal conferences to determine more precisely the pastoral methods for the proper preparation of children for confirmation.

With regard to adults, the same principles should be followed, with suitable adaptations, which are in effect in individual dioceses for the admission of catechumens to baptism and the eucharist. In particular, suitable catechesis should precede confirmation, and there should be sufficient effective relationship of the candidates with the Christian community and with individual members of the faithful to assist in their formation. This formation should be directed toward their giving the witness of a Christian life and exercising the Christian apostolate, while developing a genuine desire to participate in the eucharist (see *Introduction to Rite of Christian Initiation of Adults*, no. 19).

Sometimes the preparation of a baptised adult for confirmation is part of his preparation for marriage. In such cases, if it is foreseen that the conditions for a fruitful reception of confirmation cannot be satisfied, the local Ordinary will judge whether it is better to defer confirmation until after the marriage.

If one who has the use of reason is confirmed in danger of death, he should be prepared spiritually, so far as possible, depending upon the circumstances of the individual case.

13. Ordinarily confirmation takes place within Mass in order to express more clearly the fundamental connection of this sacrament with the entirety of Christian initiation. The latter reaches its culmination in the communion of the body and blood of Christ. The newly confirmed should therefore participate in the eucharist which completes their Christian initiation.

If the candidates for confirmation are children who have not received the eucharist and are not admitted to their first communion at this liturgical celebration or if there are other special circumstances, confirmation should be celebrated outside Mass. When this occurs, there should first be a celebration of the word of God.

It is fitting that the minister of confirmation celebrate the Mass or, better, concelebrate the Mass, especially with the priests who may join him in the administration of the sacrament.

If the Mass is celebrated by someone else, it is proper that the bishop preside over the liturgy of the word and that he give the blessing at the end of Mass.

Emphasis should be given to the celebration of the word of God which begins the rite of confirmation. It is from the hearing of the word of God that the many-sided power of the Holy Spirit flows upon the Church and upon each one of the baptized and confirmed, and it is by this word that God's will is manifest in the life of Christians.

The saying of the Lord's Prayer by the newly confirmed with the rest of the people is also of very great importance, whether during Mass before communion or outside Mass before the blessing, because it is the Spirit who prays in us, and in the Spirit the Christian says "*Abba*, Father."

14. The pastor should record the names of the minister, those confirmed, parents and sponsors, and the date and place of confirmation in a special book. The notation in the baptismal register should also be made according to law.

15. If the pastor of the newly-confirmed person is not present,

the minister should promptly inform him of the confirmation, either personally or through a representative.

IV. ADAPTATIONS IN THE RITE OF CONFIRMATION

16. In virtue of the Constitution on the Sacred Liturgy (art. 63b), episcopal conferences have the right to prepare a title in particular rituals corresponding to this title of the Roman Pontifical on confirmation. This is to be adapted to the needs of individual regions so that, after confirmation of their action by the Apostolic See, the ritual may be used in the territory.

17. The episcopal conference will consider whether, in view of local circumstances and the culture and traditions of the people, it is opportune:

a) to make suitable adaptations of the formulas for the renewal of the baptismal promises and professions, either following the text in the rite of baptism or accommodating these formulas to the circumstances of the candidates for confirmation;

b) to introduce a different manner for the minister to give the sign of peace after the anointing, either to each individual or to all the newly confirmed together.

18. The minister of confirmation may introduce some explanations into the rite in individual cases, in view of the capacity of the candidates for confirmation. He may also make appropriate accommodations in the existing texts, for example, by expressing these in a kind of dialogue, especially with children.

When confirmation is given by a minister who is not a bishop, whether by concession of the general law or by special indult of the Apostolic See, it is fitting for him to mention in the homily that the bishop is the original minister of the sacrament and the reason why priests receive the faculty to confirm from the law or by an indult of the Apostolic See.

V. PREPARATIONS

19. The following should be prepared for confirmation:

a) vestments for the celebration of Mass, for the bishop and for the priests who concelebrate with him; if the bishop does not celebrate the Mass, he and the priests who may administer confirmation with him should participate in the Mass wearing the vestments for confirmation: alb, stole, and, for the minister of confirmation, cope; these vestments are also worn for confirmation outside Mass;

b) chairs for the bishop and the priests who assist him;

c) vessel or vessels of chrism;

d) Roman Pontifical or Ritual;

e) preparations for Mass and for communion under both kinds, if it is given in this way;

f) preparations for the washing of the ministers' hands after the anointing.

Rite of Confirmation within Mass

LITURGY OF THE WORD

20. *The liturgy of the word is celebrated in the ordinary way. The readings may be taken in whole or in part from the Mass of the day or from the texts for confirmation in the* Lectionary for Mass *(nos. 763–767) and listed below (nos. 61–65).*

SACRAMENT OF CONFIRMATION

PRESENTATION OF THE CANDIDATES

21. *After the gospel the bishop and the priests who will be ministers of the sacrament with him take their seats. The pastor or another priest, deacon, or catechist presents the candidates for confirmation, according to the custom of the region. If possible, each candidate is called by name and comes individually to the sanctuary. If the candidates are children, they are accompanied by one of their sponsors or parents and stand before the celebrant.*

If there are very many candidates, they are not called by name, but simply take a suitable place before the bishop.[21]

HOMILY OR INSTRUCTION

22. *The bishop then gives a brief homily. He should explain the readings and so lead the candidates, their sponsors and parents, and the whole assembly to a deeper understanding of the mystery of confirmation.*

---

[21] *Author's footnote:* This individual calling out of the candidates is rarely performed even when very few candidates are being confirmed. This is a pity, for it has the value of personalising the sacramental form from the very beginning of the sacramental rite. The more frequent provision of confirmations for smaller groups of candidates at any one time could easily remove the practical difficulties of implementing this rubric in full. Even with larger numbers where it would be impossible to call all the candidates up onto the sanctuary, it is still desirable to call out their names and for the candidates to make some response, e.g. by standing up when their names have been mentioned.

He may use these or similar words:
On the day of Pentecost the apostles received the Holy Spirit as the Lord had promised. They also received the power of giving the Holy Spirit to others and so completing the work of baptism. This we read in the Acts of the Apostles. When Saint Paul placed his hands on those who had been baptised, the Holy Spirit came upon them, and they began to speak in other languages and in prophetic words.

Bishops are successors of the apostles and have this power of giving the Holy Spirit to the baptised, either personally or through the priests they appoint.

In our day the coming of the Holy Spirit in confirmation is no longer marked by the gift of tongues, but we know his coming by faith. He fills our hearts with the love of God, brings us together in one faith but in different vocations, and works within us to make the Church one and holy.

The gift of the Holy Spirit which you are to receive will be a spiritual sign and seal to make you more like Christ and more perfect members of his Church. At his baptism by John, Christ himself was anointed by the Spirit and sent out on his public ministry to set the world on fire.

You have already been baptised into Christ and now you will receive the power of his Spirit and the sign of the cross on your forehead. You must be witnesses before all the world to his suffering, death, and resurrection; your way of life should at all times reflect the goodness of Christ. Christ gives varied gifts to his Church, and the Spirit distributes them among the members of Christ's body to build up the holy people of God in unity and love.

Be active members of the Church, alive in Jesus Christ. Under the guidance of the Holy Spirit give your lives completely in the service of all, as did Christ, who came not to be served but to serve.

So now, before you receive the Spirit, I ask you to renew the profession of faith you made in baptism or your parents and godparents made in union with the whole Church.

Appendix II

RENEWAL OF BAPTISMAL PROMISES[22]

23. *After the homily the candidates stand and the bishop questions them:*

Do you reject Satan and all his works and all his empty promises?

The candidates respond together: I do.

Bishop: Do you believe in God the Father almighty, creator of heaven and earth?

Candidates: I do.

Bishop:

Do you believe in Jesus Christ, his only Son, our Lord,
who was born of the Virgin Mary,
was crucified, died, and was buried,
rose from the dead,
and is now seated at the right hand of the Father?

Candidates: I do.

Bishop:

Do you believe in the Holy Spirit,
the Lord, the giver of life,
who came upon the apostles at Pentecost
and today is given to you sacramentally in confirmation?

Candidates: I do.

Bishop:

Do you believe in the holy catholic Church,
the communion of saints, the forgiveness of sins,
the resurrection of the body, and life everlasting?

Candidates: I do.

---

[22] *Author's footnote:* The formulae for renewing the baptismal promises as given in the text of the rite are not completely satisfactory for young children. However, the general introduction to the rite also permits the use of the other texts given in the rite of baptism or other specially adapted texts 'more suited to the circumstances of the candidates for confirmation' (section 17(a)).

The bishop confirms their profession of faith by proclaiming the faith of the Church:
This is our faith. This is the faith of the Church.
We are proud to profess it in Christ Jesus our Lord.
The whole congregation responds: Amen.

For This is our faith, *some other formula may be substituted, or the community may express its faith in a suitable song.*

THE LAYING ON OF HANDS
24. *The concelebrating priests stand near the bishop. He faces the people and with hands joined, sings or says:*
My dear friends:
in baptism God our Father gave the new birth of eternal life
to his chosen sons and daughters.
Let us pray to our Father
that he will pour out the Holy Spirit
to strengthen his sons and daughters with his gifts
and anoint them to be more like Christ the Son of God.

All pray in silence for a short time.
25. *The bishop and the priests who will minister the sacrament with him lay hands upon all the candidates (by extending their hands over them). The bishop alone sings or says:*
All-powerful God, Father of our Lord Jesus Christ,
by water and the Holy Spirit
you freed your sons and daughters from sin
and gave them new life.
Send your Holy Spirit upon them
to be their Helper and Guide.
Give them the spirit of wisdom and understanding,
the spirit of right judgment and courage,
the spirit of knowledge and reverence.
Fill them with the spirit of wonder and awe in your presence.
We ask this through Christ our Lord.
R7 Amen.

THE ANOINTING WITH CHRISM[23]

26. *The deacon brings the chrism to the bishop. Each candidate goes to the bishop, or the bishop may go to the individual candidates. The one who presented the candidate places his right hand on the latter's shoulder and gives the candidate's name to the bishop; or the candidate may give his own name.*

27. *The bishop dips his right thumb in the chrism and makes the sign of the cross on the forehead of the one to be confirmed, as he says:*
N., be sealed with the Gift of the Holy Spirit.
The newly confirmed responds: Amen.
The bishop says: Peace be with you.
The newly confirmed responds: And also with you.

28. *If priests assist the bishop in conferring the sacrament, all the vessels of chrism are brought to the bishop by the deacon or by other ministers. Each of the priests comes to the bishop, who gives him a vessel of chrism.*

The candidates go to the bishop or to the priests, or the bishop and priests may go to the candidates. The anointing is done as described above (no. 27).

29. *During the anointing a suitable song may be sung. After the anointing the bishop and the priests wash their hands.*[24]

GENERAL INTERCESSIONS

30. *The general intercessions follow, in this or a similar form determined by the competent authority.*
Bishop:
My dear friends:
let us be one in prayer to God our Father
as we are one in the faith, hope, and love his Spirit gives.

---

[23] *Author's footnote:* In some places the bishop says the following words personally to each candidate before he anoints them:
Bishop: N. is it your will that you should be confirmed in the faith of the Church which we have all professed with you?
Candidate: It is.

[24] *Author's footnote:* It should be noted that the sacred chrism is now left on the candidate's forehead. It is not wiped off immediately afterwards by an assistant priest as before.

Deacon or minister:
For these sons and daughters of God,
confirmed by the gift of the Spirit,
that they give witness to Christ
by lives built on faith and love:
let us pray to the Lord.
R/ Lord, hear our prayer.

Deacon or minister:
For their parents and godparents
who led them in faith,
that by word and example they may always encourage them
to follow the way of Jesus Christ:
let us pray to the Lord.
R/ Lord, hear our prayer.

Deacon or minister:
For the holy Church of God,
in union with N. our pope, N. our bishop, and all the bishops,
that God, who gathers us together by the Holy Spirit,
may help us grow in unity of faith and love
until his Sons returns in glory:
let us pray to the Lord.
R/ Lord, hear our prayer.

Deacon or minister:
For all men,
of every race and nation,
that they may acknowledge the one God as Father,
and in the bond of common brotherhood
seek his kingdom,
which is peace and joy in the Holy Spirit:
let us pray to the Lord.
R/ Lord, hear our prayer.

Bishop:
God our Father,
you sent your Holy Spirit upon the apostles,
and through them and their successors
you give the Spirit to your people.

May his work begun at Pentecost
continue to grow in the hearts of all who believe.
We ask this through Christ our Lord.

LITURGY OF THE EUCHARIST

31. *After the general intercessions the liturgy of the eucharist is
celebrated according to the* Order of Mass, *with these exceptions:*
    a) *the profession of faith is omitted, since it has already been
    made;*
    b) *some of the newly confirmed may join those who bring gifts to
    the altar;*
    c) *when Eucharistic Prayer I is used, the special form of* Father,
    accept this offering *is said.*

32. *Adults who are confirmed, their sponsors, parents, wives and
husbands, and catechists may receive communion under both kinds.*

BLESSING

33. *Instead of the usual blessing at the end of Mass, the following
blessing or prayer over the people is used.*

God our Father
made you his children by water and the Holy Spirit:
may he bless you
and watch over you with his fatherly love.
R̅ Amen.

Jesus Christ the Son of God
promised that the Spirit of truth
would be with his Church for ever:
may he bless you and give you courage
in professing the true faith.
R̅ Amen.

The Holy Spirit
came down upon the disciples
and set their hearts on fire with love:
may he bless you,

keep you one in faith and love
and bring you to the joy of God's kingdom.
R̷ Amen.
The bishop adds immediately:
May almighty God bless you,
the Father, and the Son, + and the Holy Spirit.
R̷ Amen.

PRAYER OVER THE PEOPLE
Instead of the preceding blessing, the prayer over the people may be used.
    The deacon or minister gives the invitation in these or similar words:
Bow your heads and pray for God's blessing.
    The bishop extends his hands over the people and sings or says:
God our Father,
complete the work you have begun
and keep the gifts of your Holy Spirit
active in the hearts of your people.
Make them ready to live his Gospel
and eager to do his will.
May they never be ashamed
to proclaim to all the world Christ crucified
living and reigning for ever and ever.
R̷ Amen.
The bishop adds immediately:
And may the blessing of almighty God,
the Father, and the Son, + and the Holy Spirit,
come upon you and remain with you for ever.
R̷ Amen.

Texts for Mass at the Celebration of Confirmation

1. MASS PRAYERS

A

Entrance Antiphon: I will pour clean water on you and I will give you a new heart, a new spirit within you, says the Lord.

Opening Prayer
God of power and mercy,
send your Holy Spirit to live in our hearts
and make us temples of his glory.

or
Lord,
fulfil your promise.
Send your Holy Spirit to make us witnesses before the world
to the good news proclaimed by Jesus Christ our Lord,
who lives and reigns with you and the Holy Spirit,
one God, for ever and ever.

Prayer over the Gifts
Lord,
we celebrate the memorial of our redemption
by which your Son won for us the gift of the Holy Spirit.
Accept our offerings
and send us your Spirit
to make us more like Christ
in bearing witness to the world.

When Eucharistic Prayer I is used, the special form of Father, accept this offering *is said:*
Father, accept this offering
from your whole family
and from those reborn in baptism
and confirmed by the coming of the Holy Spirit.
Protect them with your love and keep them close to you.

Communion Antiphon: All you who have been enlightened, who have experienced the gift of heaven and who have received your share of the Holy Spirit: rejoice in the Lord.

Prayer after Communion
Lord,
help those you have anointed by your Spirit
and fed with the body and blood of your Son.
Support them through every trial
and by their works of love
build up the Church in holiness and joy.

B

Entrance Antiphon: The love of God has been poured into our hearts by his Spirit living in us.

Opening Prayer
Lord,
send us your Holy Spirit
to help us walk in unity of faith
and grow in the strength of his love
to the full stature of Christ,
who lives and reigns...

Prayer over the Gifts
Lord,
you have signed our brothers and sisters
with the cross of your Son
and anointed them with the oil of salvation.
As they offer themselves with Christ,
continue to fill their hearts with your Spirit.

Communion Antiphon: Look up at him with gladness and smile; taste and see the goodness of the Lord.

Prayer after Communion
Lord,
you give your Son as food
to those you anoint with your Spirit.
Help them to fulfil your law
by living in freedom as your children.

May they live in holiness
and be your witnesses to the world.

OTHER MASS PRAYERS
These may be used in place of those given above:

Opening Prayer
Lord,
fulfil the promise given by your Son
and send the Holy Spirit
to enlighten our minds
and lead us to all truth.

Prayer over the Gifts
Lord,
accept the offering of your family
and help those who receive the gift of your Spirit
to keep him in their hearts
and come to the reward of eternal life.

Prayer after Communion
Lord,
we have shared the one bread of life.
Send the Spirit of your love
to keep us one in faith and peace.

2. READINGS

The following readings are given in the official lectionary for
use in the celebration of this sacrament. It would be very
fitting for the candidates and their teachers to select the
readings for their own confirmation Mass from this list.
Where the local bishop is willing to allow this to be done, it
can provide yet one further way in which they can participate in the celebration of this sacrament. The usual procedure should be followed of selecting an Old Testament
reading, a psalm, a New Testament reading, an Alleluia
verse (optional), and a gospel reading.

Text for Mass

OLD TESTAMENT READINGS
1. Isaiah 11: 1–4 The Gifts of the Spirit.
   The Spirit brings new life and growth.
2. Isaiah 42: 1–3 The Spirit of gentleness and of justice.
   The Spirit is given to God's chosen servant.
3. Isaiah 61: 1–3, 6, 8–9 The Spirit and the 'Good News'.
   The Spirit inspires people to bring healing, freedom and joy to others.
4. Ezekiel 36: 24–8 The Spirit of renewal.
   The Spirit is 'within' God's people, bringing them a renewal of their lives and the forgiveness of their sins.
5. Joel 2: 23, 3: 1–3 The universality of the giving of the Spirit.
   The Spirit is to be 'poured out' on the whole world, and is the cause of great rejoicing.

NEW TESTAMENT READINGS
1. Acts 1: 3–8 The Promise of the Spirit.
   'The Spirit will inspire you to be my witnesses to the ends of the earth.'
2. Acts 2: 1–6, 14, 22–3, 32–3 The 'outpouring' of the Holy Spirit.
   The Pentecost story and the first sermon of St Peter.
3. Acts 8: 1, 4, 14–17 The work of the Holy Spirit.
   Peter and John lay hands on the people of Samaria after their baptism.
4. Acts 10: 1, 33–4, 37–44 The descent of the Holy Spirit on Cornelius.
   The sermon of St Peter after the baptism of Cornelius and his household in which he testifies to the way Christ was anointed with the Spirit during his life-time, and is now exalted in glory.
5. Acts 19: 1–6 The work of the Holy Spirit.
   St Paul lays hands on the people of Ephesus after their baptism.
6. Romans 5: 1–2, 5–8 The Spirit of Love.
   When Christ died on the cross, God demonstrated his great love

113

for sinful man, and poured out his love on all mankind through the Holy Spirit which is given to them.

7. Romans 8: 14–17 The Spirit of adoption.
   The Spirit leads people to become true children of God.

8. Romans 8: 26–7 The Spirit of Prayer.
   The Spirit guides people to pray to God as 'Father'.

9. I Corinthians 12: 4–13 The different 'ministries' of the Spirit.
   Wisdom, power of expression, healing, miraculous powers, prophecy, discernment, 'tongues' and their interpretation, are all exercised within one body, one community under the guidance of the Spirit.

10. Galatians 5: 16–17, 22–3, 24–5 The Fruits of the Spirit.
    Living by the Spirit, following the Spirit.

11. Ephesians 1: 3, 4, 13–19 The Seal of the Spirit.
    God chose his people before time began, and he enlightens them with the spirit of wisdom and insight and of faith.

12. Ephesians 4: 1–6 The unity of the Spirit.
    The Spirit will guide God's people to live in peace with each other and with faith and hope in God.

THE RESPONSORIAL PSALMS
1. Psalm 21.
2. Psalm 22.
3. Psalm 95.
4. Psalm 103.
5. Psalm 116.
6. Psalm 144.

The Lectionary should be consulted for the exact editing of these psalms, and for the various responses which are given. The same is true of the Alleluia Verses.

THE GOSPEL READINGS
1. Matthew 5: 1–12 The Christian spirit.
   The Beatitudes: the confirmed Christian must commit himself to poverty, gentleness, justice, mercy, and peace.

2. Matthew 16: 24–7 The spirit of self-denial.
   The confirmed Christian must be ready to take up his cross and follow Christ.
3. Matthew 25: 14–30 The spirit of eagerness.
   The Parable of the Talents: the confirmed Christian must use his talents wisely and well.
4. Mark 1: 9–11 The descent of the Spirit on Jesus.
   The baptism of Jesus as the 'servant of God.'
5. Luke 4: 16–22 The Spirit of Christ.
   The visit of Jesus to the synagogue at Capernaum.
6. Luke 8: 4–10, 11–15 The spirit of growth and of new life.
   The Parable of the Sower: the confirmed Christian must always be ready to receive the word of God into his heart.
7. Luke 10: 21–4 In praise of the Spirit.
   The gift of true wisdom is given to the poor and to children.
8. John 7: 37–9 The Spirit and life.
   The Spirit brings life to God's people – like the life-giving water of the rivers.
9. John 14: 15–17 The promise of the Spirit.
   'I will ask the Father to send you an advocate.'
10. John 14: 23–6 The Spirit is our teacher (1).
    'The Spirit will instruct you, and remind you of all I have said.'
11. John 15: 18–21, 26–7 The Spirit is our teacher (2).
    'The Spirit bears witness to the goodness of Christ.'
12. John 16: 5–7, 12–13 The Spirit is our teacher (3).
    'The Spirit will guide you into all truth.'

MUSIC

'Attention should be paid to the festive and solemn character of the liturgical service and its significance for the local Church especially if all the candidates are assembled for a common celebration.' (General introduction, section 4.)

One obvious way of emphasizing the festive and solemn character of the ceremony of confirmation is through the use of music and singing, which also encourages the candidates and their families and friends to take a fuller part in the celebration. For the most part the following list merely draws attention to the usual places where the congregation can participate through singing, but it includes two additional occasions in the ceremony of confirmation itself where the rite suggests the use of singing.

INTRODUCTORY RITES
Entry Song
Penitential Rite
Gloria

THE LITURGY OF THE WORD
Responsorial Psalm[25]
Alleluia
(the Creed is not said)

THE RITE OF CONFIRMATION
The Renewal of the Baptismal Promises
   In place of the words 'This is our faith', the community may express its faith in a suitable song (Rite, section 23)
During the Anointing
   A suitable song may be sung at this point (Rite, section 29)[25]

THE LITURGY OF THE EUCHARIST
Offertory Song
Sanctus
Acclamation after the Consecration
      (N.B. – The Children's Eucharistic Prayers also include several other acclamations.)
The Doxology and Amen

THE COMMUNION RITE AND THE DISMISSAL
The Communion Rite and the Dismissal
Our Father
Lamb of God
Communion Song[25]
Recessional

   [25] At these points it would be desirable to make additional use of a choir to provide variety and interest and a suitably meditative atmosphere.

'Come, Holy Spirit'

A bible service in preparation for the celebration of the sacrament of confirmation

NOTE: There are innumerable ways of putting together a service such as the one that follows. The example given is only a suggestion, and can obviously be shortened or adapted to suit individual circumstances. Where there is sufficient time and facilities available, the various prayers given in Part One and Two could be recomposed by the pupils themselves, on similar lines, but in a more personal style. Also the story of the Pentecost Reading could be given a more imaginative presentation through mime or drama.

For convenience the 'celebrant' is named throughout this ceremony as the priest, obviously, however, the ceremony could equally well be performed under the direction of a teacher or catechist.

INTRODUCTION
Sign of the Cross

The celebrant introduces the ceremony in these or similar words:
For quite a long time you have now been preparing for the sacrament of confirmation At last you are approaching the time when the bishop of the diocese is to come to celebrate the confirmation Mass.

When that day comes, the bishop will stretch out his hands over you, and anoint you with oil, as a sign of the 'Gift of the Holy Spirit' that is given to you. Long ago when the disciples of Christ were waiting for the Holy Spirit to come down on them, they spent many hours together in prayer, asking God to bless them with his help. Let us also pray to God like them, asking him to strengthen us and make us more like his Son, Jesus Christ, our Lord.

Appendix IV

PART ONE
WE RECEIVE THE GIFTS OF THE HOLY SPIRIT SO THAT WE MAY HELP OTHERS

HYMN

Any hymn or song about the work of the Holy Spirit, but especially one which mentions the Christian duty to care for others.

Celebrant:

At confirmation the bishop anoints each candidate with chrism on the forehead, making the sign of the cross in oil as he does so. This is a sign that God is strengthening each of the candidates so that they may serve God in the way he has chosen. When we are anointed at our confirmation, this is a sign that we too have been chosen for the service of God and given a job of work to do. Let us therefore begin our prayers today by asking God to forgive us for not serving him as well as we could have done in the past and promising to do better in the future.

Child 1: Jesus, we are sorry
if sometimes we forget how much you love us.
Jesus, we are sorry
if we are selfish,
if we refuse to share your love with other people.
Help us to live in peace and harmony with others in future.
Lord, have mercy.
R̷ Lord, have mercy.

Child 2: Jesus, we are sorry
if sometimes we have been filled with anger
even with hatred towards others.
Help us to bring happiness to others in the place of
arguments and fighting.
Lord, have mercy.
R̷ Lord, have mercy.

Child 3: Jesus, we are sorry
if sometimes we spoil things.

Help us to make things better, not worse.
Lord, have mercy.
℞ Lord, have mercy.

Child 4: Jesus, we are sorry
if sometimes we hurt each other by what we say.
Help us not to be cruel to others by the words we use.
Lord, have mercy.
℞ Lord, have mercy.

Child 5: Jesus, we are sorry
if sometimes we refuse to listen to others,
if sometimes we refuse to show consideration to others,
even though we expect them to be good to us.
Help us to treat others as we would like them to treat us.
Lord, have mercy.
℞ Lord, have mercy.

Everyone then says the following words all together.
Lord, help us to know, love and serve you better ourselves,
so that we can help others to follow you,
and may we all live together in peace and harmony.

PART TWO
WE PROMISE TO BECOME
MORE LIKE CHRIST

HYMN

Any hymn or song that emphasizes the duty of each Christian to follow in the footsteps of Christ.

Celebrant:

The power of the Holy Spirit that you will receive at confirmation is very real. You may not be able to 'feel' it or 'see' it, but this should not make you doubt its effect on your lives. After all you cannot see or feel the electricity that surges through the wires in this building. When you plug something into the mains, you cannot see the electricity pouring out of the plug into your record player or into the electric drill.

But you can still be absolutely sure that the electricity will make your record player work when you switch it on, and the same with the drill. In a similar way you can be absolutely sure that Jesus Christ will give you a second 'outpouring' of the Holy Spirit at confirmation, to strengthen you as one of his followers. He did this for his disciples on the first Pentecost Sunday, and you can be certain that he will do the same for you. Listen now to the story of that day as it is told in the Acts of the Apostles:

READING

Acts 2: 1–21 *should be read at this point.*
(*There is a version of this passage on pp. 43-4 above.*)

HOMILY

If a homily is to be given, it should be a very brief one, ending in these or similar words:
At confirmation the bishop will extend his hands over all those to be confirmed. He will ask God to bless us with the 'gifts of the Holy Spirit'.

Child 6: God our Father, give us a spirit of wisdom.
Father, we pray that your Holy Spirit will help us
to make wise decisions in life,
so that we may always love you
and try to help others.
Lord, hear us.
All: Lord, graciously hear us.

Child 7: God our Father, give us a spirit of understanding.
Father, we pray that your Holy Spirit will help us
to be tolerant and forgiving towards others
just as you are towards us.
For you are kind and merciful
to both the good and the bad alike.
Lord, hear us.
All: Lord, graciously hear us.

Child 8: God our Father, give us a spirit of right judgement.
Father, we pray that your Holy Spirit will help us
to recognize good from bad.
Help us especially to understand the wisdom of Christ
and to follow his teaching.
Lord, hear us.
All: Lord, graciously hear us.

Child 9: God our Father, give us a spirit of courage.
Father, we pray that your Holy Spirit
will give us the courage to do what Christ wants us to do,
even when this is hard and difficult.
For we have been called to follow in the footsteps
of the great saints and martyrs of long ago.
Lord, hear us.
All: Lord, graciously hear us.

Child 10: God our Father, give us a spirit of knowledge.
Father, we pray that your Holy Spirit
will help us to see just how good you are to us
so that we may always appreciate
your goodness and your kindness.
Lord, hear us.
All: Lord, graciously hear us.

Child 11: God our Father, give us a spirit of reverence.
Father, we pray that your Holy Spirit
will help us always to show you
the honour and respect that you deserve from us.
Lord, hear us.
All: Lord, graciously hear us.

Child 12: God our Father, give us a spirit of wonder and awe
in your presence.
Father, you are the Lord of life.
You are great and do wonderful things.
With the help of your Holy Spirit
may we all come to know something of your greatness and
your glory.

Lord, hear us.
All: Lord, graciously hear us.

All then say the following words together:
May the Holy Spirit bless us
by giving us a greater share in his holy gifts.
May we all be filled with a spirit of wisdom and understanding,
of right judgement and of courage,
of knowledge and of reverence,
and of wonder and awe in the presence of God.

The celebrant then says:
This Holy Spirit, who blessed and strengthened the first disciples of Christ, will very soon come to you in a special way to give you an increase of his help. But even now, even before we have been confirmed, the Holy Spirit helps us. When we cannot find the right words to use, the Holy Spirit encourages us to turn to God in prayer full of confidence, and to call God 'Our Father'. Let us now join together in prayer to God our Father and say:
All: Our Father...

The celebrant continues:
When we were baptised, our parents and godparents promised that they would help us to become true followers of Christ. Since then we have all tried in our own ways to put this into practice and to become true Christians. Through our daily prayers and our kindness to others we have tried to become faithful followers of Our Lord. Let us pray that with the help of the Holy Spirit to guide us we may become even more like Christ.

THE BLESSING
The ceremony can end with the Blessing (or the Prayer over the People) from the confirmation Mass.
Hymn: Any hymn or song of thanks and praise.

Preparing the Parents and Sponsors of Candidates and the Local Parish

PARENTS

It is important for parents of young candidates to be fully involved in the preparation for this sacrament and in the lead-up immediately before it. Obviously there are many ways of achieving this depending on the resources of the parish or school through which the candidates are being prepared. This appendix concentrates on the way parish clergy and especially the school chaplain can assist in this work. Much of what is suggested here, however, could equally well be done by others.

The simplest way of involving parents is by the school chaplain visiting them in their own homes. Though time-consuming, it is particularly useful with the most retiring parents who are unwilling to ask questions in a public meeting. An alternative to this is to gather parents together in small discussion groups on a local basis – but this may only be practical in these areas where discussion groups are already flourishing. The other alternative is to invite all the parents to a public meeting at the school or in the parish hall for a talk about the sacrament followed by questions and, hopefully, also discussion.

Whatever approach is followed, parents should be given adequate notice of the fact of the forthcoming celebration of the sacrament. It is still common practice in some areas to arrange and publicise confirmations at the last moment, only a week or two before the ceremony is to take place. Candidates and their parents should not have to put up with this kind of treatment.

The following letter was sent to parents of all the children eligible for confirmation at one particular school. It gives some idea of the way in which parents could be drawn into the preparations at an early stage.

St Richard's Junior High School,
Marfleet Lane, Kingston upon Hull.
5th February 19

Dear Parent,

Preparation for the Sacrament of Confirmation

Last year the Clergy of East Hull decided that children attending St Richard's Junior High School should be confirmed during the last term of their fourth year at the school. Your child is now eligible to receive this sacrament during this present year, and we would like to know whether or not you wish to have your child prepared for confirmation.

Confirmation is a sacrament which continues the work begun at baptism. At baptism your child became a member of God's Church. By now he or she should have a reasonable knowledge of the faith, and should have shown a willingness to put it into practice. We will therefore expect each of the children themselves to show that they want to be confirmed and are ready to attend any extra periods of instruction which prove necessary to complete their preparation for this sacrament.

Each child will be confirmed in his or her own parish by the bishop under the direction of your own parish priest during the last week in July of this year. Exact dates will be announced very shortly.

It is very important that you return the slip below to the school if you would like your child to be confirmed.

Yours sincerely,

A. J. McCallen   T. J. P. Ryan
(School Chaplain)   (Headmaster)

NAME OF PUPIL.................... PARISH............

ADDRESS ....

I would like my SON/DAUGHTER to be prepared for confirmation.

Signed ....
Parent or Guardian.

Please detach and return to school as soon as possible.

The amount of material to be covered in discussions with parents will depend entirely on the parents themselves and on the style of meeting chosen. Most parents will at least want to know about the practical details of the ceremony: time and place; seating arrangements (will the candidates sit together with their sponsors, or will they be able to stay with their families throughout?); the dress of the candidates (slightly older girls may object strongly to wearing white dresses. Even school uniforms, if available, may be unpopular); who can be a sponsor? (parents themselves may present their own children for confirmation now); special confirmation names (it is no longer necessary for children to choose a second saint's name at confirmation, their baptismal saint's name will suffice). All these items are important and should not be overlooked.

If possible parents should also be encouraged to think more deeply about the nature and purpose of the sacrament. Generally speaking people tend to fall into two groups: those who know nothing about the sacrament and those who already have fairly fixed views about it, especially those who see it as a sacrament of growing-up.

The first group includes the non-catholic partners of mixed marriages, but it also numbers those who remember nothing of their own confirmation – and there are a remarkably large number of these. For them a short run-through the rite itself offers the best way of getting the greatest amount of information in the most clear and direct fashion. The prayers of the rite are not extensive and the same is true of the signs and actions used, but they provide more than enough concentrated material even for a fairly light-weight discussion.

The second group includes those who for various reasons believe that confirmation is nothing less than the specific occasion when their children become adult Christians. For them a more thoughtful discussion of the sacrament may be called for. Many of these would want to defer the sacrament until a very much later stage when their children are 'ready for it'. This may demand some kind of examination of the history of the sacrament explaining how the Church has arrived at its present position, and showing how confirmation belongs with baptism and is not intended to be a distinct sacrament of spiritual adulthood. The discussion of spiritual adulthood may also call for a wide ranging investigation of teenage psychology and of the religious attitudes and practice of young people. But in the end the discussion should come back to the words and actions of the rite itself and to the fundamental nature of the rite as a celebration of the outpouring of the Holy Spirit at Pentecost through which the candidate receives a further share in the transforming life of the Spirit and so becomes (gradually) more like Christ.

SPONSORS

The General Introduction to the Rite of Confirmation gives a fairly detailed consideration of the role of sponsors in sections 5–6. This could well be read in full by those intending to act as sponsors (see p. 95).

Further information will be found in the teaching material given above on pp. 24–26.

The following words are taken from *Confirmation: helping Catholic Parents* (CTS 1972) translated from the French of *La Diffusion Catechistique* (Lyon).

The Church recommends that as far as possible each child should be assisted on his confirmation day by a sponsor.

At the moment when the bishop confirms the child, the sponsor should put his hand on the shoulder of the boy or girl, vouching for him or her, so to speak, both now and for the future.

Choose a man or woman who is a whole-hearted Christian – not just a practising Christian but a convinced Christian, someone who will really be able to help the child.

Choose someone young enough to be able to understand the child and follow his progress in the years to come. Rather than a family relative living some distance away, it would be better to choose someone living in the neighbour-hood or the parish, someone who is known to the parents and familiar to the child. That will make for easier confidence between them. It would be a good idea to choose the sponsor some time before the confirmation: this will give the relationship more chance of lasting.

The sponsor is not simply an elegant appendage to the confirmation ceremony. What the Church is looking for is a genuine Christian who will feel responsible with the parents for the child's faith and will give him real help.

PARISH

Confirmation is or has been a somewhat neglected sacrament. Yet the celebration of confirmation in a parish or within a deanery should be an important local event. Especially where there are several people to be confirmed in a particular place, it is good for the local Church to pray for the candidates, e.g. by including a special bidding prayer for this intention at Mass on the day of the ceremony and perhaps also on the previous Sunday. The time and the place of the ceremony should be well publicised, and members of the local parish should both know what is happening and feel welcome to come if they wish.

The eve of the confirmations is an excellent occasion on which to hold a penitential service specifically geared to the candidates themselves but open to their parents and families and to the parish in general. This could even become a suitable opportunity for the granting of a general absolution where this is permissable.

Work Sheets for those Preparing for Confirmation[26]

CHAPTER 1
MY CONFIRMATION

page 25

(1) a) my name is .....
    b) I was called after Saint .....   [Christian name]
    c) I was born on .....   [date]
    d) I was born at .....   [place]

(2) a) I was baptised and became a member of God's family
    on .....   [date]
    b) at .....   [place]
    c) by .....   [the person who baptised you]
    d) my godparents were .....

(3) a) I first went to confession at ..... [place]
    b) I first received our blessed Lord
    in Holy Communion at .....   [place]
    c)   on .....   [date]

(4) a) I now live in the parish of .....
    b) the priests who look after our parish are ...../.....

(5) a) I am going to be confirmed
    on .....   [date]
    b) at .....   [place]
    c) by .....   [name of bishop]
    d) my sponsor will be .....   [name]
    e) when I am confirmed, it will be ..... years since I
    first became a follower of Christ at baptism.
    f) my confirmation name will be .....

Note (*1*) *Sponsors*
You need one sponsor to present you for confirmation. It

[26] These are gathered here for the convenience of the teacher. The page references are to the original position of these work sheets in the text.

would be a good idea if this person was the same as one of your godparents at baptism, but any other suitable person can take their place, including your own parents.

The sponsor must be a member of the Catholic Church. They must be baptised and confirmed and have made their first holy communion. They should also be sufficiently mature for this responsibility. It is best if your sponsor can be present at your confirmation.

Note (2) Confirmation Names
It is not necessary to choose a special 'confirmation name' – the 'Christian name' you normally use can be used at confirmation so long as it is a saint's name. But if you do choose a special name for your confirmation, this must be a saint's name, and you should have a good reason for choosing it.

CHAPTER 2
GOD IS OUR FATHER

page 27
At baptism the priest asks the parents of each child to renew the promises of their own baptism. This is the first of the questions he asks:

'Do you believe in God, the Father almighty, creator of heaven and earth?'

The parents answer 'I DO'.
At confirmation the bishop asks the candidates to answer the same question for themselves, and they reply 'I DO' in the same way.

page 30
1. *Who is God the Father?*

God the Father of our Lord Jesus Christ
has created us, and gives us life.
He loves us all, and cares for us,
for he is the Father of all his People.

2. What must I do to please God the Father?
    I must love God
        with all my heart,
        with all my soul,
        with all my strength,
        and with all my mind;
    and I must love my neighbour
    as much as myself.

3. If God our Father has created us, and still takes care of us, then we, at least, should be ready to return the love he has shown to us. We can do this in our prayers to him, and in our acts of kindness to others.

CHAPTER 3
JESUS CHRIST

page 32

At baptism the priest asks the parents of each child to renew the promises of their own baptism. This is the second of the questions he asks.

  'Do you believe in Jesus Christ,
  his only Son, our Lord,
  who was born of the Virgin Mary,
  was crucified, died, and was buried,
  rose from the dead,
  and is now seated at the right hand of the Father?'
  The parents answer 'I DO'.

At confirmation the bishop asks the candidates to answer the same question for themselves, and they reply 'I DO' in the same way.

page 36

1. *Who is Jesus Christ, our Lord?*
    Jesus Christ is the Son of God,
    he always was the Father's Son,
    but he was born on earth and died for us
    so that we might be raised up from our sins
    and share his life with God for ever.

2. Dying you destroyed our death,
   rising you restored our life,
   Lord Jesus, come in glory.

3. Day by day,
   O dear Lord, three things I pray,
   to see thee more clearly,
   love thee more dearly,
   follow thee more nearly,
   day by day.

4. If Jesus has suffered and died for us,
   then we, at least, should be ready to get to know him
      better
   and to follow him.

CHAPTER 4
THE HOLY SPIRIT IS OUR HELPER AND GUIDE

page 38

At baptism the priest asks the parents of each child to renew the promises of their own baptism. This is the third of the questions he asks.

'Do you believe in the Holy Spirit?'
The parents reply 'I DO'.

At confirmation the bishop asks the candidates to answer the same questions for themselves. Because confirmation is the special 'sacrament of the Holy Spirit', he asks this question in a slightly different way, as follows:

'Do you believe in the Holy Spirit,
the Lord, and giver of life,
who came upon the apostles at Pentecost
and today is given to you sacramentally in confirmation?'

The candidates reply 'I DO'.

page 43

PENTECOST

Before Pentecost: the disciples prayed to God the Father for help and guidance.

Appendix VI

At Pentecost: God the Father 'poured out the gift of the Holy Spirit' on the disciples to give them the power and the strength that Jesus had promised them.

After Pentecost: The disciples began to do what Christ himself had done. They became 'more like Christ', ready and able to continue his work in the world as members of the community of the Church.

page 49
The gifts of the Holy Spirit
Wisdom: to help us to be truly wise and to follow the way of God.

Understanding: to help us to see things as God sees them

Right judgement: to help us to recognize what is good and what is bad according to the Law of God.

Courage: to help us to follow the way of God bravely whatever the difficulties or hardships this may demand.

Knowledge: to help us to recognize the goodness and greatness of God and to appreciate his kindness to us.

Reverence: to help us to show God the love, honour, and respect he deserves from us.

Wonder and awe: to help us to appreciate something of the glory of God.

page 49
The fruits of the Holy Spirit
Love and joy
Peace and patience
Kindness and goodness
Faithfulness, gentleness and self-control.

page 51
Who is the Holy Spirit?
The Holy Spirit is 'the Gift of God'
who shares his life with all mankind.
He guides us, and he strengthens us
to help us all to follow Christ with faith and love
in the unity of his holy Church.

CHAPTER 5
A CHURCH OF SAINTS

page 54

At baptism the priest asks the parents of each child to renew the promises of their own baptism. This is part of the last of the questions he asks them:

'Do you believe in the holy catholic Church,
the communion of saints, the forgiveness of sins,
the resurrection of the body and life everlasting?'
The parents reply 'I DO'.

At confirmation the bishop asks the candidates to answer the same question for themselves, and they reply 'I DO' in the same way.

page 56
Our diocese, our bishop
I
a What is the name of your bishop . . . . .
b Where does he live . . . . .
c Where was he born . . . . .
d When was he ordained priest . . . . .
e Where did he work as a priest . . . . .
f When was he ordained bishop . . . . .
g Have you ever seen the bishop . . . . .
  if so, where . . . . .
h Try and find a photograph of your bishop from a newspaper etc. and put it in your work book.

II
a What diocese does your area belong to . . . . .
b Where is the cathedral of your diocese . . . . .
c Give a list of the parishes in your area . . . . .
d Draw a simple map of your diocese, giving the main towns etc.

A prayer from the confirmation Mass (from the bidding prayers) about the bishop:

Let us pray for the holy Church of God,
in union with N. our Pope, N. our Bishop and all the Bishops,
that God, who gathers us together by the Holy Spirit,
may help us grow in unity of faith and love
until his Son returns in glory.

page 57
What is a saint?

1. What is a saint?

    Write an answer to this question in twenty words.
    Some suggestions: the word 'saint' is sometimes used to describe all of the following – though obviously in different ways.

    any member of God's family who has been baptised
    any member of God's family living with him in heaven
    any member of God's family whose life has been carefully investigated by the Church, and has been canonized, because they are exceptionally good and especially worthy of being imitated.

2. Name five saints who have been canonized by the Church. Then briefly explain why the Church should want us to follow their example.

3. a Write down your own 'Christian' name .....
    (note: a 'Christian' name is the name of the saint after whom you were called).
    b Explain briefly what this saint was famous for .....

4. a Write down your sponsor's 'Christian' name .....
    b Try and find out your sponsor's confirmation name and write this down also .....

5. It is not necessary to choose another saint to be your patron saint at confirmation. You do not have to choose a new 'confirmation' name. But if you decide to do so,

write down your new name, and explain briefly what your
new patron saint was famous for.

page 59
One of the prayers taken from the Blessing at the end of the
confirmation Mass, which emphasises the work of each
Christian as a member of the Church, is this:
> Jesus Christ the Son of God
> promised that the Spirit of truth
> would be with his Church for ever:
> may he bless you and give you courage
> in professing the true faith.

Another prayer of blessing from the end of the confirmation
Mass, which underlines the same point:
> God our Father,
> complete the work you have begun
> and keep the gifts of the Holy Spirit
> active in the hearts of your people.
> Make them ready to live his gospel
> and eager to do his will.
> May they never be ashamed
> to proclaim to all the world Christ crucified
> living and reigning for ever and ever.

CHAPTER 6
THE SACRAMENT OF CONFIRMATION

page 63
At baptism the priest asks the parents of each child to renew
the promises of their own baptism. He asks them if they are
prepared to reject sin and to live as God's children, using the
following three short questions:
> 'Do you reject sin so as to live in the freedom of God's
> children?
> Do you reject the glamour of evil and refuse to be mastered
> by sin?

Do you reject Satan, Father of sin and prince of darkness?'
To each of these questions the parents answer 'I DO'.

At confirmation the bishop asks the candidates if they are
prepared to reject sin and to live as God's children, but on
this occasion he does so using one question only as follows:
'Do you reject Satan and all his works
and all his empty promises?'
The candidates reply 'I DO'.

page 65
At baptism our parents and godparents say and do everything
for us.
But in confirmation:
When the bishop says 'Do you believe?'
WE say 'I DO', not our parents.
When the bishop says 'BE SEALED WITH THE GIFT OF
THE HOLY SPIRIT'.
WE say 'AMEN'.

At confirmation we repeat our baptismal promises in public
to show that we really are 'children of God'
to show
that we ourselves want to obey God and
to help other people to do the same
that we ourselves want to follow Christ and
to help other people to follow him
that we ourselves want to live as faithful members of his
Church and
to help other people to live in the
same way.

At baptism we became members of God's family 'in the name
of the Father and of the Son and of the Holy Spirit.' At
baptism we *began* our lives as Christians. We became 'like
Christ'.

The Church pictures baptism as our first meeting with Christ. At baptism we are like the first disciples of Christ who met him for the first time down by the sea in Galilee.

At confirmation we receive the 'seal of the gift of the Holy Spirit'. At confirmation we are *strengthened* as Christians and become '*more* like Christ'.

The Church pictures confirmation in terms of the 'out-pouring of the Holy Spirit' at Pentecost. At confirmation we are like the followers of Christ who waited in the Upper Room for him to send down on them the Spirit of power and understanding. They were already 'friends of Christ' – they had been the followers of Christ for several years, and many of them had been working closely with Christ teaching others about the Good News and even working miracles. But now Christ was no longer visible to them, they received a new 'outpouring of the Holy Spirit' to *help them to continue* the work of Christ. Jesus did not leave them 'alone'. He kept the promise he had made to them before his death. And his 'gift' to them of the Holy Spirit gave them all the help and support they needed.

The following prayer, taken from the confirmation Mass, emphasizes this 'outpouring' of the Holy Spirit which we receive at confirmation.

My dear friends,
in baptism God our Father gave the new birth of eternal life
to his chosen sons and daughters.
Let us pray to the Father
that he will pour out the Holy Spirit
to strengthen his sons and daughters with his gifts
and anoint them to be more like Christ the Son of God.

Appendix VI

page 68
Growing up as followers of Christ

1. Give at least four ways in which you have changed since you first came to this school (or over the last four years if this is longer).

    e.g. how much taller are you .....
    how much heavier .....
    any difference in your hair style .....
    any difference in your style of clothes .....
    do you live in the same house .....
    any other ways in which you have changed .....

    Try and remember what you were like four years ago and compare this with what your are like now.

2. These outward signs of growth and development are important, but other less obvious 'changes' (e.g. in our attitudes or in our abilities) are even more important.

    Give at least four ways in which you have changed 'in yourself' over the last four years – especially in your attitudes or interests:

    e.g. have you the same friends .....
    have you improved in sport .....
    have you become interested in different sports .....
    have you become more interested or less interested in your work at school .....
    do you do the same things in your free time .....
    what do you do that's different .....
    do you spend your money on the same things .....
    what different things do you spend your money on .....
    do you treat your parents differently .....
    in what way .....
    do you treat your teachers differently .....
    in what way .....

3. Do you think there has been any change or development in yourself as a 'follower of Christ' over the last four years .....

    Try and describe this in about twenty words .....

CHAPTER 7
THE SACRAMENT OF CONFIRMATION

page 72
Christ the prophet
Jesus calls men to love and serve God the Father.

Throughout his life
and especially through his death and resurrection
he proclaimed the loving kindness of God the Father.

We follow in the footsteps of Christ,
for we have been called by God
to love and serve him.
Through our baptism and our confirmation
we become more like to Christ
so that we can help others to follow him.

Christ the priest
Jesus offered himself to God on our behalf.

Throughout his life
and especially through his death and resurrection
he dedicated himself to God the Father
as a perfect sacrifice of love and praise.

We follow in the footsteps of Christ,
for we have been called by God
to offer him everything that is good in our lives
Through our baptism and our confirmation
we become more like to Christ
so that we can share in his perfect sacrifice.

Christ the king
Jesus is the King of the Universe.
Throughout his life
and especially through his death and resurrection
he established the kingdom of God
of justice, peace and truth and love.

We follow in the footsteps of Christ,
for we have been called by God
to make his kingdom grow on earth.
Through our baptism and our confirmation
we become more like to Christ
so that we can help to build the kingdom
of justice, peace, and truth and love.

page 74
The oil of chrism and the anointing of each candidate
What connection has oil with the following?
Vaseline? .....
    What is it used for? .....
Athletes? .....
    What is it used for? .....
Lamps? .....
    What is it used for? .....
Fires? .....
    What is it used for? .....
Machines (e.g. cars)? .....
    What is it used for? .....

page 74
In the sacrament of confirmation we receive the gift of the
Holy Spirit to help us to continue the work of Christ.
We receive:
    the health and the strength of the Holy Spirit
    the light (and the understanding) of the Holy Spirit
    the warmth (and the love) of the Holy Spirit
    the power (the 'driving force') of the Holy Spirit.

page 75
The 'seal' of the Holy Spirit
As the bishop 'anoints' each candidate with chrism he says
the following words,
    'Be sealed with the **Gift** of the Holy Spirit'.

Confirmation Work Sheets

page 76
The 'sign' of the cross
When the bishop 'seals' each candidate with holy chrism, he does so by making the sign of the cross in oil on the forehead of each of those to be confirmed, as a reminder to them of the death of Christ on the cross.

page 77
The 'imposition of hands'
At confirmation, just before he anoints each candidate, the bishop (and all the other priests who are assisting him) extend their hands over the people to be confirmed. While they do this, the bishop says the following prayer:

All powerful God, Father of our Lord Jesus Christ,
by water and the Holy Spirit
you freed your sons and daughters from sin
and gave them new life.
Send your Holy Spirit upon them
to be their helper and guide.
Give them the spirit of wisdom and understanding,
the spirit of right judgement and courage,
the spirit of knowledge and reverence.
Fill them with the spirit of wonder and awe in your
presence.
We ask this through Christ our Lord.

Then, as he anoints each candidate, the bishop performs an individual 'imposition of hands' by making the sign of the cross on the forehead in chrism.

page 80
The sign of peace
After the anointing with chrism the bishop says to each candidate, 'Peace be with you', and gives them a sign of peace. Each candidate replies in a clear voice, 'And also with you'.

page 81
The following words are taken from one of the Bidding Prayers of the confirmation Mass:

Let us pray to the Lord for all men
of every race and nation,
that they may acknowledge the one God as Father,
and in the bond of common brotherhood
seek his kingdom
which is peace and joy in the Holy Spirit.

CHAPTER 8
THE CONFIRMATION MASS

page 83
The people present at the confirmation Mass
The bishop
The priests of the parish
The people to be confirmed
The sponsors
Parents and friends
Members of the parish

What does the bishop do?
He will extend his hands over all those to be confirmed
and pray for them.
He will sign you with the cross in chrism, and say,
'(Peter or Mary etc.) be sealed with the Gift of the Holy
Spirit'.
He will give you the 'sign of peace', and say
'Peace be with you'.

What do you do?
You will take a full part in the Mass, especially by listening
to what is said and by joining in the hymns and the responses.
You will renew you baptismal vows along with the
other candidates,
and when the bishop says, 'Do you believe...?'
you will say 'I DO' clearly and distinctly.
You will go forward with your sponsor to receive the sign of
the cross in chrism on your forehead.
When the bishop says 'Be sealed with the Gift of the Holy
Spirit' you will reply 'AMEN'.
When the bishop gives you the sign of peace and says 'Peace
be with you' you will reply 'AND ALSO WITH YOU'.